No Freedom Without Regulation

No Freedom Without Regulation

The Hidden Lesson of the Subprime Crisis

JOSEPH WILLIAM SINGER

Yale

UNIVERSITY PRESS

New Haven and London

Yale University Press books may be purchased in quantity for educational, business, or promotional use. For information, please e-mail sales.press@yale.edu (U.S. office) or sales@yaleup.co.uk (U.K. office).

Designed by Sonia L. Shannon.
Set in PMN Caecilia type by IDS Infotech, Ltd.
Printed in the United States of America.

Library of Congress Control Number: 2015930742
ISBN 978-0-300-21167-2 (cloth : alk. paper)

A catalogue record for this book is available from the British Library.

This paper meets the requirements of ANSI/NISO Z39.48-1992 (Permanence of Paper).

10 9 8 7 6 5 4 3 2 1

Where there is no Law,
there is no Freedom.

—JOHN LOCKE

Contents

I

The Subprime Challenge

All that makes existence valuable to anyone
depends on the enforcement of restraints upon the
actions of other people.

JOHN STUART MILL

Sherlock Holmes and Dr. Watson go on a camping trip.
They set up their tent, have a modest repast, and go
to sleep. In the middle of the night, Holmes wakes
Watson up and asks him, "What do you see?" Watson
looks up and sees the night sky and tells Holmes so. "What does
it mean?" Holmes asks. Pondering this deep question, Watson
answers, "It means the universe is vast and mysterious and our
knowledge limited. It means that we only understand what we
can observe and that—" Holmes interrupts him. "No, you idiot,"
he says. "It means someone has stolen our tent."[1]

Things That We Have Taken for Granted

Sometimes it is important to state the obvious, to confront
truths so fundamental we have forgotten to see them. The subprime crisis has forced us to remember things that we have

taken for granted. Here is the most important lesson from the subprime crisis: neither private property nor the free market can exist without law. Another word for "law" is "regulation." That means that *neither private property nor the free market can exist without regulation.* Markets are defined by a legal framework that sets minimum standards for social and economic relationships. Private property is possible because law allocates property and defines the rights of owners; property law also ensures that property rights are not exercised in ways that harm the property or personal rights of others or that undermine the fabric of social life or economic prosperity.

These things are true but they are not well understood. Consider this puzzle. The subprime crisis happened because of inadequate regulation of financial transactions. Yet the main political movement that emerged from the crisis was the Tea Party—a group hell-bent on reducing the size of government. Why did a crisis brought on by inadequate regulation result in a political movement that abhors government? The answer is that Americans are trapped by an ideology that sees government as the enemy of freedom, and regulation as an interference with both the free market and private property. Both conservatives and liberals conceptualize regulation as a limitation of market freedoms and as an infringement on the rights of owners. But this idea, pervasive though it may be, is incoherent and pernicious. The truth is that we would have neither markets nor private property nor freedom without law. And "regulation" is simply another word for "the rule of law."

The Tea Party revolt of 2013 shut down the federal government and nearly caused the United States to default on its debt payments. The shutdown began as an attempt to overturn the Affordable Care Act (or "Obamacare"), but the underlying message was one of general contempt for "government." The rhetoric was overheated and intense; according to Senator Ted Cruz, we were facing a grand battle between those who hate government and love freedom on the one hand and those who love government and hate freedom on the other. Obamacare, he said, was an example of "force and coercion from government" and he was against it because "I value my freedom." He explained that "the free market works and government regulation does not."[2] Senator Cruz did not argue for the abolition of government. Yet his rhetoric suggested that any regulation by government is inherently bad both because it interferes with freedom and because it imposes costs on the private sector that impede job creation and prosperity.[3]

Libertarians like Senator Cruz strike a chord with many Americans because we do value liberty and no one likes being told what to do. And "regulations" do seem to interfere with our freedom to act as we please. But libertarians are not anarchists; they do not want the complete abolition of government. What they oppose is regulation. What do they mean by this? Libertarians of a philosophic bent argue that law should be limited to preventing force and fraud, enforcing contracts, and protecting the rights of property owners.[4] The problem is that it is not easy to define what it means to do these things and no more.

The subprime crisis teaches us this lesson. Were subprime mortgages freely negotiated contracts or were they procured by fraud and deception? How should we interpret what their terms actually were? Did those agreements constitute an exercise of property rights or a deprivation of them? Or both? The subprime crisis reminds us that, even if we adopt a libertarian value framework and seek to minimize government regulation of both markets and property, we would still need a great deal of "regulation" to do the work a supposedly minimal state requires. Allocating and defining the rights of owners is not a simple task, nor is determining when a contract has been formed and what its terms are.

Regulation turns out to be essential both to markets and to property. This is true whether one is a libertarian or a liberal. The question is not whether to rely on the free market or on government regulation; that is a false choice. The question is, what legal framework for property and markets best enables us to exercise our liberties in a manner consistent with the values of a free and democratic society that treats each person with equal concern and respect and works to promote our legitimate interests?

It is hard to remember these basic truths because most Americans are stuck in a paradigm that treats markets and regulations as mortal enemies. Alan Greenspan, for example, had long argued that markets work well without regulation and that regulations designed to fix market imperfections inevitably fail.[5] In the midst of the subprime debacle, when Greenspan testified before Congress on October 23, 2008, Representative Henry Waxman noted that this was the reason Greenspan had refused to act to "prevent irresponsible lending practices that led to the subprime crisis" even though Greenspan had had the authority to do so.[6] Greenspan admitted that there was a "flaw" in the model that he had long used to define "how the world works," and that he now understood that free markets have limitations and that regulations might be needed to prevent catastrophic market failures.[7]

Libertarians like Greenspan are not the only ones who contrast markets and regulations. Even a liberal economist like Joseph Stiglitz frames the issue this way. In writing about the subprime crisis, for example, Stiglitz wrote that "markets do not work well on their own," that "[g]overnment needs to play a role ... in regulating markets," and that "[e]conomies need a balance between the role of markets and the role of government."[8]

Framing the issue as the correct balance between "the free market" and "government regulation" distorts our understanding of both concepts. For one thing, this way of framing the issue wrongly suggests that markets can exist without a legal framework. For another thing, it wrongly suggests that all regulations interfere with both liberty and property rights. But Greenspan's pre-subprime worldview was flawed not because markets can be imperfect and not because government regulations sometimes succeed in ameliorating those imperfections. It was flawed because neither markets nor private property can exist at all without regulation.

The freedoms markets enable to flourish exist because regulations make markets possible. Similarly, private property exists because law structures and protects the rights of owners. The free market is not anarchy; it is a regulatory structure that requires detailed laws to set the rules of the game. And property owners are not warlords; they do not have despotic power over those who enter their property. The law protects and limits the rights of owners to ensure that property rights are compatible with individual freedoms, including market freedom.

The foreign minister of Czechoslovakia, Jiri Dienstbier, commented in 1990, "[i]t was easier to make a revolution than to write 600 to 800 laws to create a market economy."[9] If anything, this is a vast understatement. Both markets and property are enabled by law; without law, they do not exist. And creating a viable legal structure for both is a complicated business.[10] Rules are needed not only to establish general principles; the legal system must develop ways to deal with hard cases, and those are far more numerous than non-lawyers may imagine. The specifics matter; when it comes to the law governing the market economy, God is indeed in the details.

The notion that markets and regulations are antithetical is a deeply incoherent idea. Similarly, the idea that regulations necessarily impair the rights of owners cannot withstand scrutiny. Indeed, it is impossible to protect owners without regulations that stop others from interfering with those owners' rights, and that requires laws that define what the rights of owners are—a much harder thing to do than we may assume.

The idea that markets and regulation are opposites is a remarkably tenacious one, despite many pieces of evidence to the contrary.[11] The Great Depression convinced nearly everyone that government regulation was necessary to enable markets to work, not just well, but at all. When the subprime crisis hit, it was apparent that the rules of the game governing the market needed to be fixed. It was also obvious that property rights are vulnerable if they are not protected by appropriate regulations.

Nevertheless, we continually hear claims that the government should not interfere with market mechanisms.[12] Like Senator Cruz, presidential candidate Mitt Romney argued in 2011 that "[t]he right course is to let markets work . . . We need to get government out of the way."[13] The idea that "regulation" interferes with "the free market" is like a phoenix that cannot die. It keeps getting reborn. Why is that?

Freedom and Law

The answer has to do with the way Americans conceptualize what it means to be free. Regulatory laws often prevent us from doing things we might want to do; they interfere with our freedom to act as we please. Conservatives and liberals alike believe that we each have the right to "pursue happiness."[14] This means that (within limits) we should be free to choose how to live our lives. Markets are one way we promote and exercise this kind of freedom. But freedom of action without limits is not liberty. Regulations may seem to deny us freedom, but regulation is just another word for "the rule of law." Conservatives revere freedom, and one of their champions is John Locke. But it was Locke who taught us that "where there is no Law, there is no Freedom."[15] What does it mean to say that law promotes freedom? It means

7

that markets are not a war zone. Rather, they are defined by laws that establish rules of the game. Conservatives cannot be against regulation and for markets because markets do not exist without law.

Market enthusiasts sometimes forget the benefits of law. In their enthusiasm for liberty, they take law for granted. Conservatives use the word "regulation" to mean "bad laws." They are indeed right that some laws are either counterproductive or downright harmful. But that means we need to identify which laws are bad. When that is the case, then the question is not *whether* to regulate markets at all, but how to figure out *which laws* are needed to support legitimate market structures. When we treat markets and regulations as opposites, it is hard to see the ways in which appropriate regulations enable markets to work. If we understood this relationship, it might be easier to find more common ground between liberals and conservatives.

Our current polarized political rhetoric makes it hard for us to see that liberals and conservatives agree upon a lot more than we may think they do. If we remember that conservatives value law, we will see that conservatives believe in regulation as much as liberals do. Conversely, if we remember that liberals value free choice as much as conservatives do, we will see that liberals believe in markets as much as conservatives do. Both liberals and conservatives believe in free markets and private property, and both agree that freedom of action must be constrained by law. The deeper truth is that laws designed to allow us to live together in harmony do not take away our liberty; they are what make us free. Regulations needed to define market structures and property rights are not intrusions on private liberties; they are the rules of the game that enable both to exist and to work both well and fairly, and they are therefore protectors of our freedom.

Liberty, it turns out, is a complex concept. It embraces the notion of freedom of action, but it also is shaped by the values of security and equality. We are not free to live our own lives on our own terms unless we are secure from being harmed by others. I am not free to walk the streets if I am afraid of being assaulted or killed. That means that our individual freedom of action must be limited by laws protecting our security and ensuring our safety from harmful actions of others. Liberty is promoted both by laws allowing freedom of action and by laws limiting free actions to promote security. And because we live in a free and democratic society premised on the belief that all human beings are created equal, we cannot deny others the ability to exercise the same freedoms we demand for ourselves. That means we must curtail our actions to the extent necessary to enable others to exercise equal freedoms.

Just as liberals value freedom of action, conservatives value both security and equality. Liberty entails the right to self-determination and to be free from domination by others. Democracies are premised on the commitment to treat each human being with equal concern and respect. Equality is not only a liberal value. Conservatives fiercely champion the right of each person to enjoy liberty. That means that liberty is not just an individual concept but a social and political one. If we demand freedom and security for ourselves, we cannot deny it to others if we believe that each person is entitled to equal concern and respect. Because a free and democratic society guarantees freedom for each person, it limits the ability of individuals to act in ways that deny others equal liberty and security.

Liberty therefore requires laws that limit our freedom of action; such laws ensure that each person has an equal opportunity to pursue happiness. To shape such laws, we must attend to the ways in which the exercise of liberty by one person may infringe on the rights and liberties of others. Laws establish background rules to enable the liberty of each to be compatible with the liberty of all. Laws may limit our natural freedom to act at will but they promote political liberty—the freedom to pursue happiness in a manner that enables others to do likewise.

The fact that law promotes freedom does not mean that all laws are good; some laws indeed take away our "freedom" as we conceive it. Nor does it mean that liberals and conservatives agree on which laws are necessary to promote liberty. What it does mean is that promoting liberty requires a strategy other than "getting rid of government regulation." Freedom requires appropriate regulations that promote the way of life that allows us to enjoy our core liberties. The rule of law is not an excuse for oppressive or counterproductive rules; it is a recipe for reasonable regulations that protect our legitimate interests and basic values. Such regulations do not deny freedom; they promote it. Regulation (if it is both sensible and appropriate) supports, rather than undermines, the liberties cherished by conservatives and liberals alike.

Why Both Liberals and Conservatives
Need a New Paradigm

Given the poisonous, partisan disputes in Washington these days, one can be forgiven for thinking we are hopelessly divided by competing ideologies, values, and commitments. If, however, we reflect on the ways that law promotes freedom, we may be surprised to discover that liberals and conservatives agree on a great deal more than we might think. It is simply not true that conservatives favor markets and liberals favor regulation. The truth is that liberals also support free markets and conservatives also support regulation. What they disagree about is how to define our core liberties; doing so requires value-laden choices about the contours of our way of life. Such choices are necessary to distinguish regulations that promote freedom from those that deny it.

It is true that liberals and conservatives emphasize different values; liberals are more focused on promoting equality, and conservatives are more focused on promoting freedom of action. But it is also true that liberals value freedom of action and conservatives value equality. The overlap between liberalism and conservatism is far greater than current rhetoric or politics would suggest.

Liberals have long supported laws designed to structure markets to promote equal opportunity, fair competition, and consumer protection. But since President Reagan's libertarian philosophy came to dominate American political discourse, liberals have been walking uphill. Conservatives have engaged in a successful long-term public relations campaign to portray liberals as elitists who want to take away our liberties by denying us the freedom to do what we want to do. Few Americans want to be known as liberals. And liberals themselves sometimes do not know how to champion their own ideals, especially the ideal of equal opportunity.

Liberals know that government is necessary to create the conditions that allow each person to flourish. At the same time, liberals are in favor of markets; they simply champion laws that structure them appropriately. However, because liberals have generally accepted the conservative frame that places freedom and regulation in opposition, many liberals do not have the capacity or the language to adequately defend their own views. Where they should be confident, they are defensive. Liberals need a new way to frame questions of liberty and regulation so that they can better understand, express, communicate, and defend their views.

At the same time, conservatives have adopted a libertarian paradigm that both undermines their own ideals and makes it more difficult to develop areas of agreement with liberals. Conservatives tend to use the word "regulation" only for laws they dislike. When conservatives want regulation, they tend to justify it by calling it something other than "regulation." They may call it "preventing fraud," "enforcing contracts," "protecting property rights," or "promoting the rule of law."

Surprisingly, libertarian values championed by many conservatives support regulatory laws long favored by liberals. It is impossible to protect private property without a regulatory structure that defines property rights and sets their legitimate contours and limits. It is impossible to promote free markets or freedom of contract without rules to determine when a contract has been made, what it means when it is ambiguous, how to enforce it, and when to allow excuses for breach. It is also impossible for either markets or property to exist without laws ensuring that we treat each other with dignity, as free and equal persons. For these reasons, conservatives actually support many regulatory laws. Perhaps most surprising of all, most "liberal" regulations can be understood and defended as ways to protect both "freedom of contract" and "private property"—core conservative values.

Many conservatives recognize this. As Mitch Daniels, the former Indiana Republican governor, explained, "We [conservatives] should distinguish carefully skepticism about big government from contempt for all government."[16] Author and *Wall Street Journal* columnist Peggy Noonan agreed: "Republican politicians now often feel reluctant to move forward on regulatory bills that would have a beneficial effect and are in line with conservative thinking, because the idea of government regulation has become poisonous among the base."[17]

It is hard for all of us to see the extent to which liberals and conservatives agree on the need for regulation because we conceptualize "regulation" as denial of liberty. By overstating the evils of government and denigrating the very idea of regulation, conservatives have made it more difficult for all of us to recognize the large areas of agreement that exist between conservatives and liberals.

It is of course true that some regulations are overly intrusive, costly, or counterproductive. But that just means that the goal is sensible regulation rather than "deregulation." Choosing which laws work and promote an appropriate framework to achieve our deepest values is difficult, no matter what your political philosophy or moral compass is. It requires the exercise of judgment and practical wisdom. But we will make better judgments if we understand the ways in which both free markets and private property depend on a just and workable legal framework. That framework promotes, rather than detracts from, the values of liberty and equality. Developing a correct understanding of the relationship between "markets" and "regulation" will enable both liberals and conservatives to better express and defend their views. And it will reveal surprising amounts of agreement between what are often seen as warring camps.

All this requires nuanced thinking and the willingness to see things from another person's point of view.[18] Our polarized political discourse pushes us to reject nuance and to adopt extreme positions. Such rhetoric may make us feel good but it is a poor basis for mature thinking about public policy and law. Free markets are not possible without regulation, and regulations cannot work if they do not take into account human psychology, human values, and human frailties. Markets and property need regulation, and good markets and property need sensible regulation. To figure out which regulations are sensible and which are not, we need a better conception of the relationship between law and economics, between government and society, and between regulation and markets.

We need a new framework for thinking about these issues. This new paradigm can better express the ideals of liberals and conservatives alike and will reveal surprising areas of agreement between them. That consequence, in turn, could furnish a new basis for negotiation and compromise between our warring political parties. I am not naïve enough to think that a few clever sentences can turn political enemies into friends, but I am hopeful enough to believe there is reason to try.

The Role of Property

Property has been at the center of our national problems for the last few years. The subprime mortgage market has not only scarred the world economy but confronted us with the colossal consequences of both bad business practices and bad laws. The subprime crisis dramatizes the ways in which the institution of private property depends on regulation. Inadequate or inappropriate regulations led both to individual hardship and to collective disaster. Without a workable legal framework, property cannot exist. Jeremy Bentham was right when he said, "Property and law are born together, and die together. Before laws were made, there was no property; take away laws, and property ceases."[19]

Our property law system regulates the packages of property rights that people can create. Because we tend to view regulation as a deprivation of freedom, many react skeptically to these sorts of legal rules. But after the subprime crisis, it will never again be difficult for me to explain to my property law students why property rights need a viable legal structure and why some bundles of property rights should not be created at all. The law regulates property rights for many reasons, and one of them is to prevent people from creating property rights that impose hardships on other people.

The subprime crisis taught us this crucial lesson. Securitized subprime mortgages not only affected those who entered these transactions; they were toxic assets that wrecked the world economy. The property transactions we engage in may have large effects on others, including those who were not party to our transactions. We each seek the freedom to do what we like on our own land and with our own property, but that does not mean we have the right to engage in actions that pollute the land of our neighbors. We may want to create tailored mortgage transactions that suit our purposes and needs, but that does not give us the right to invent property arrangements that undermine the foundations of economic life and the security of everyone's property titles.

Just as we tend to oppose "the free market" and "government regulation," we tend to view all regulations as interferences with "private property" or the "rights of owners." This way of framing the relationship between property and regulation makes it difficult to see that private property is not possible without law. And the law necessary to have a working private property system is complicated and vast.[20] If it were easy to describe the legal structure of private property, law schools would not teach semester-long courses on property, partnerships, corporations, wills, trusts, real estate transactions and finance, negotiable instruments, banking, secured transactions, copyright, patents, bankruptcy, family law, land use regulation, and environmental law. Nor could we simplify the law and get rid of all these sets of rules; the problems they solve would still exist, and we would be forced either to re-create all these areas of law or to live in a world dramatically less pleasant than our own.

It turns out that complex normative and practical judgments are needed to define the scope of property rights, the contexts within which they operate, and the rules by which they are developed and transferred. We need to "regulate" property to ensure it is preserved, useable, and marketable so that the use of property by one person does not unduly impinge on the property and personal rights of others. We need property law to clarify titles, to protect justified expectations, and to prevent abuses of the rights of others. Just as markets are not possible without "regulation," private property cannot exist without a robust regulatory infrastructure. There is no private property without law, and that means that regulation supports, rather than undermines, property rights.

Of course that is an overstatement. Regulation may be necessary in general but that does not mean that specific regulations are desirable. It is indeed the case that some regulations unnecessarily and unjustly impinge on the justified expectations of owners. Libertarians may seek to get rid of all regulations that interfere with "established property rights," but the truth is that if we got rid of all such regulations, libertarians would soon demand that we replace them. That is because "unregulated" property is an oxymoron.

A factory that causes air and water pollution and harms neighbors by making their properties toxic and their bodies cancer-ridden is not merely exercising its own property rights. It is destroying the property and personal rights of others. The freedom to use property must be limited to protect the property and security of others. The landlord who refuses to rent to someone because of her race may be exercising her property rights, but she is preventing others from acquiring property. We prohibit race discrimination in housing not because we do not care about protecting property rights, but because we want them to be available to everyone.

Our recent experience with subprime mortgages—and subprime laws—should lead us to a new appreciation of the regulations we might have taken for granted. It also reminds us of how much we depend on well-functioning markets and the ways in which laws contribute to both markets and property rights. Liberals and conservatives alike could benefit from an enlightened understanding of the ways the rule of law shapes and protects property rights and market freedoms while promoting liberty, equality, prosperity, and democracy.

Democratic Liberty

To answer the challenge of creating a new paradigm for thinking about the relationship between markets and regulation, I offer the concept of *democratic liberty*. We live in a free and democratic society premised on the core values of liberty, equality, and democracy. That means we aspire to treat each person with equal concern and respect, to give each person the freedom to live life on his or her own terms as long as those are compatible with the rights and liberties of others, and to enable the people to use democratic processes to govern themselves and to define and protect their basic rights.

If we think about what it means to live in a free and democratic society, it becomes clear that all social and economic relationships must be subject to minimum standards regulations to enable each person to exercise freedom in a manner consistent with the freedom of others. It also becomes clear that one of the ways we exercise freedom is to choose leaders who enact laws that set those minimum standards. Relationships that fall below those minimum standards are banned; they are *subprime*. Freedom does not mean doing whatever we like; it means collectively and freely adopting laws that enable us to live with others in harmony and prosperity. We do what we like within boundaries adopted through democratic means. Freedom entails government of the people, by the people, and for the people. The liberty we cherish is not the absence of regulation; it is the freedom to live with others under rules we have adopted together and which set the minimum standards that enable us—each of us—to pursue happiness.

Chapter 2 explains why regulation is essential to both freedom and democracy. One of the underlying causes of the subprime crisis was the failure of bankers and other market actors to understand the benefits of regulation. Rather than making money within prevailing legal rules and practices, the banks evaded them. Our national penchant to demonize "regulation" is an underlying factor in explaining how the subprime crisis happened. I will argue that, far from interfering with our liberty and property rights, regulation is just another word for the rule of law, and a free and democratic society needs law.

We can better see this truth by looking at history. The freedoms cherished by conservatives and liberals alike emerged from a historical process that revolted against feudalism, aristocracy, slavery, racial segregation, and gender discrimination. Free and democratic societies outlaw market and property arrangements that are inconsistent with our conceptions of freedom and equality. Without that legal infrastructure—without those regulations—we would be neither free nor empowered to own property; nor would we have the benefits that markets give us.

Chapter 3 explains why, far from interfering with free markets, consumer protection laws are an essential foundation to economic transactions and to economic liberty. Fraudulent, unfair, or deceptive practices undermine confidence in markets; they discourage participation in market transactions and undermine the economy. Moreover, when they take the customer's property on false or misleading pretenses, they constitute a form of theft, undermining property rights and personal dignity.[21] Consumer protection regulations do not interfere with our liberty or paternalistically deprive us of choices. Nor do they inhibit "free markets." Rather, they ensure that we get what we want when we enter the market, and they free us from the fear that businesses will take advantage of us.

Markets are supposed to serve our interests by allowing us to act on our preferences so that we can get what we want. But one thing we want are laws that protect our justified expectations when we enter those market relationships. We want not only the freedom to choose the terms of our contracts but freedom from the fear of being cheated or injured by those with whom we make deals. For that reason, conservatives, as much as liberals, should favor strong consumer protection laws. Rather than limiting freedom of contract, those laws promote it; rather than infringing on the property rights of business owners, they protect the property rights of consumers. Indeed, rather than interfering with the free market, consumer protection laws enable it to work.

Chapter 4 explains why private property needs a regulatory infrastructure. Property cannot exist if we do not have relatively clear rules about who owns what. But an infrastructure also cannot operate justly if we do not ensure that property rights are not abused so as to cause harm to others. The mechanisms used to market subprime mortgages violated the justified expectations of borrowers and undermined the clarity of land titles. These subprime practices are a vivid reminder of the reasons why laws are needed to create a viable infrastructure for both markets and private property.

Chapter 5 addresses the politics of regulation and explains why liberals and conservatives share more values than we may realize. Our polarized political system and our hotly contested elections lead us to believe that we are a sharply divided nation.

And on some issues and in some respects that is obviously true. But political rhetoric has become so one-sided and extreme that our differences are exaggerated. In fact, Americans agree upon a lot more than one might think. I explain why, contrary to what we may assume, conservatives—and even libertarians—should like regulation. Regulation (or "the rule of law") is essential to both individual liberty and private property. Conservative values actually support seemingly liberal regulations that define minimum standards for both markets and property rights. Properly structured regulation promotes conservative values rather than undermines them.

I also explain why liberals should like free markets and private property. Unlike conservatives, liberals do not assume that regulation of economic life is an infringement on either our freedom or our property rights. Indeed, liberals are apt to be skeptical of both "big business" and "the free market." The subprime crisis only confirms their fears. That raises the danger that liberals may overstate their case and see markets as inherently problematic. It also may lead conservatives to assume that liberals do not favor "the free market."

Yet liberals are not against markets. They want neither a state-run economy nor prohibition of economic exchange. What they want are just markets. While properly skeptical of the unfairness that can arise in improperly regulated markets, liberals actually agree with many of the values held dear by conservatives and libertarians alike. Contrary to what we may assume, liberals champion markets. After all, liberals are enemies of feudalism just as much as conservatives are. Indeed, the idea of free choice is as much a liberal value as a conservative one.

Understanding how properly structured markets support liberal values may help liberals see the extent to which they share values that conservatives profess. It may also enable liberals to better defend their proposals in terms that conservatives can understand and support. Similarly, while liberals may worry about the have-nots, this does not mean that they do not value private property; what they value is making sure that everyone can have some. If that is so, the question is how to spread the benefits of property to more people. This is a value that conservatives share. There are good ways and bad ways to spread access to property, and subprime mortgages turned out to be one of the bad ones. But ownership is not only a conservative value; it is one that liberals should embrace. That does not mean that being a homeowner is always a better option than being a renter; it means that ensuring access to the things we need for a fulfilling human life is one of the core functions of a private property system in a free and democratic society.

This book concludes in Chapter 6 by explaining that democracies promote liberty by outlawing subprime practices that are beneath our dignity. We seek to live in a free and democratic society, and that means we need law. Our laws set *minimum standards for market relationships and for property rights*. We use democratic political means to adopt minimum standards for market and property relationships that are compatible with the norms and values of a free and democratic society. Those minimum standards ensure that we treat other individuals with equal concern and respect and that we make sure that each of us is equally free to pursue opportunity and happiness.

Conduct that falls beneath those minimum standards is *subprime*. It is the job of law—of regulation—to free us from having to worry about subprime products and arrangements. Just as our mortgage markets distinguished between prime and subprime mortgages, we need to distinguish between prime and subprime market practices. What we should be against is not "the free market" but subprime markets premised on unfair and deceptive practices. What we should be against is not "regulation" but subprime regulation that undermines freedom, equal opportunity, and prosperity. What we should be for is sensible regulation and just markets. Conservatives are quite right that regulations can be counterproductive and unnecessarily intrusive. But liberals are also right that markets can be unnecessarily destructive and counterproductive. The subprime markets taught us this hard-won lesson.

We should embrace democratic liberty. That means freedom, equality, democracy, and the rule of law. We need a legal infrastructure that works and is consistent with the values of a free and democratic society. It is true that bad laws impair our liberties and deprive us of our rightful property. We should never forget that. But sensible regulation takes away neither our freedom nor our property. Rather, regulation, properly structured, can enable every human being to become an owner, to have a home, to live a life of comfort and joy, and to make a place in the world. It is time we Americans understood that *regulation is just another word for the rule of law*. The rule of law neither degrades nor imprisons us; it makes us free. And because we are a free and democratic society, we need a political system that enables us to combine government by the people with our fundamental normative commitment to the idea that each person is free and equal. Regulation does not impede these goals; it is the way we achieve them.

2

Why a Free and Democratic Society Needs Law

No Title of Nobility shall be granted by the United States.

—U.S. CONSTITUTION ART. I, §9, CL. 8

I n the fall of 2013, the Tea Party shut down the federal government and nearly caused the United States to default on its debt payments. The rhetoric was overheated and intense. It seemed we were facing a grand battle between opposing philosophies. On the right, we had those who hate government and love freedom, and on the left we had those who love government and—and what? Hate freedom? What was striking about the debate over the shutdown was the lack of normative confidence on the left. We heard exhortations to pay our bills, to enforce the law, and to allow the government to do its work of protecting the public. What we did not hear was a connection between government and freedom.

We are stuck in a paradigm that sees government action as coercive and individual action as freedom. Government seems to protect our security by administering insurance programs like Social Security, Medicare, and unemployment benefits, by protecting us from foreign enemies, and by preventing us from harming each other. What is not evident is how government and government regulation promote liberty. Even liberals do not know how to talk about government as a bulwark of freedom rather than as its enemy.

Where does government come from? If all it does is take our liberty away, why did we establish it in the first place? Our national consciousness rests on a fable invented by Thomas Hobbes and John Locke.[1] That myth suggests that, in the beginning, there was no government. Human beings were free to do what they pleased. One of the things that pleased people was to harm others and steal their stuff. Because we were vulnerable to harm, we banded together in a social contract to create government to protect our lives, liberties, and property. This myth is buttressed by tales of hearty Americans who went west and settled on open lands, worked them, and established property rights. They did not need government's help to do any of this. Government followed and has been meddling in their lives ever since.

These origin stories appear to justify limited government. They do so because they depict it as a necessary evil, coming after the fact, to protect us from harm from bad people. Government appears as an interloper. We would rather have our natural liberty; we would rather not have to pay taxes to protect ourselves from bad people. We grudgingly created government to protect us from harm; the laws government enacts accomplish this by limiting our liberty to protect our security.

These twin stories of natural liberty and western settlement are reassuring. But they are entirely mythological. They are neither historically accurate nor normatively plausible. The truth of the matter is that our form of government did not spring from the state of nature or the Wild West. It did not emerge from nothing. It came into being because we Americans rejected the kinds of governments that had gone before. We decided to abolish both monarchy and titles of nobility. We decided to abolish hereditary offices and dictatorial edicts. Democracy came about by rejecting aspects of the prior regime that are inconsistent with the idea that "all men are created equal" and that we are endowed with rights to "life, liberty, and the pursuit of happiness." Nor were we the first to rebel against or to reform a prior regime that was experienced as inimical to freedom. Constitutional government in Great Britain, for example, emerged from a long historical process that got rid of the most objectionable aspects of feudalism while retaining monarchy and lordship.

If we look at actual history rather than Lockean or American myths, we will see that the liberties cherished by conservatives and liberals alike required government regulations that abolished feudalism and slavery. The freedom we espouse requires *outlawing* property and contract rights that are characteristic of indentured servitude and feudal fealty. We live in a free and democratic society, and such societies are premised on the fundamental values of liberty, equality, and democracy. Because we are committed to treating others with dignity and because we believe in self-determination, we have laws that prohibit the creation of relationships incompatible with our most cherished values.

Understanding our actual history teaches us how regulation is necessary both to promote freedom and to enjoy and protect property. But it also enables us to see that conservatives and liberals agree upon a great deal more than one might think from reading current news about our polarized political parties. Americans may say they hate "regulation," but they also strongly support liberty, equality, and democracy.

American democracy is an enormous human achievement. It happened not because we rejected regulation; it happened because we embraced laws prohibiting servitude and subordination. It happened because we outlawed property arrangements and contractual relationships incompatible with the values of a free and democratic society that treats each person with equal concern and respect. The freedoms we cherish did not come from deregulation; we enjoy them *only because of regulation.*

The Conventional Story About the Rise of Government and Private Property

Americans are taught from an early age that settlers moved west and built farms and homes, thereby establishing property rights. In this conventional story, government is missing. If government enters the story at all, it follows settlers, protecting them by enacting laws preserving the fruits of their labor. Government is an afterthought rather than a constitutive actor.

This story is ingrained in the American psyche. It comes not only from folk tales, but from the fictional history of property taught to us by Thomas Hobbes and John Locke.[2] According to that legend, first there was a "state of nature" without government or law. Private property as we understand it did not exist; land was owned either by no one (Hobbes's view) or by everyone in common (Locke's view). Private property came into existence only when individuals banded together with others to create a social contract to protect farmers from having their crops stolen by bandits after months of grueling labor.

In Locke's view, property rights preexisted the state, which came into being only to protect previously acquired rights. In Hobbes's view, property rights exist only if they have legal protection and thus come into being only with the advent of law and governmental protection. In either case, it is the actions of individuals, who enclose open land and devote it to farming or grazing purposes, that constitute the origin of property rights. But those rights are vulnerable to attack in the state of nature. The social contract that led to the state made property rights secure by granting them legal protection. Whether property rights preexist the state or not, only a sovereign state with a functioning legal system can ensure that property rights are not merely ephemeral.

Most property law professors tell a similar tale, identifying first possession as the origin of property rights.[3] The most common way to teach this principle is through the case of *Pierson v. Post*.[4] In that case, two hunters quarrel over who owns a fox; was it the hunter who had chased the fox all day and was on the verge of overtaking it, or the hunter who intervened and shot the fox first? Property law gives the right to the one who first "captured" the fox by shooting it and mortally wounding it.

Both property law professors and economists also widely reference the work of Harold Demsetz, who argued that property rights arose to avoid the "tragedy of the commons."[5] Common ownership of a field or forest can lead individuals to seek to take what they can from the land before others take it. This will produce a race to get the land's resources ahead of the others and may lead to overuse that may destroy the land. Each individual benefits from taking as much as possible as soon as possible; if you wait, others will take as much as they can and there will be nothing left for you. Although this practice may decrease the value of the land, individuals have no incentive to moderate their uses to maximize the long-run potential of the land. Those who do not act quickly lose everything. Although it makes sense from a social standpoint to use the land wisely, individuals acting rationally will overuse the land to obtain what they can in the short run. In contrast, granting an owner property rights in a parcel of land forces that owner to internalize the costs of overuse, potentially leading to an efficient use of resources. Property rights are thus said to increase social welfare because they give owners incentives to maximize the value of the land.

All these stories assume that there is enough land for everyone so that giving individuals rights to exclude others from their land will not leave others homeless and without opportunities of their own. If people are free to "go west" and take the land they need, then the only legitimate role of government is to protect owners from invasion or harm. Government regulation of property does nothing but interfere with the freedom to do what you want with your own land.

This conventional story is charming but false. Here is what really happened.

The Rise and Fall of Feudalism in England

Edward the Confessor was far from the worst king in English history, but he did commit the unpardonable sin of dying without an heir and being less than clear about establishing a successor.[6] William the Conqueror, also known as the Bastard, claimed that Edward had promised him the crown, but on his deathbed Edward appeared to have named Harold Godwinson to succeed him. After Harold was crowned, William crossed the English Channel from Normandy to seize the crown from him. After defeating Harold's army and killing him and his brothers at the Battle of Hastings, William was crowned King on Christmas Day of 1066. Shortly afterward, King William built the White Tower, a structure that still sits in the middle of the Tower of London. From that base of operations, he methodically conquered England.

Within a few years, William had dispossessed almost all the English lords and replaced them with his trusted men. In so doing, William claimed ownership of all of England and parceled out rights to pieces of it to his lords in return for obligations to provide him knights to defend the realm from enemies foreign and domestic or to provide him religious services to protect the kingdom and his own soul. Those lords, in turn, "subinfeudated" by making arrangements with tenants who would provide the services the lords needed in return for access to land. Those sublords, or vassals, found tenants of their own, and so on. At the bottom of the feudal ladder were the peasants who lived on and worked the land. And below the bottom were the serfs ("villeins")—euphemistically called "unfree"—who were essentially slaves.[7]

The feudal system was complex, and it varied throughout England and changed over time. In important respects, however, it was far different from the social and legal environment that we associate with "the free market" and is, or should be, anathema to conservatives and liberals alike. There was nothing like full ownership of land in this system. Rather, everyone was tied to everyone else by personal relationships of allegiance and loyalty. No one was free in our modern sense of the word.

Lords pledged fealty to the Crown, and tenants pledged fealty to lords. This meant tenants agreed not only to carry out specific obligations but, in general, to do the lord's bidding.[8] There were customary limits on what the lords could demand of tenants, but a tenant was not independent; he was the lord's man. Nor could tenants easily move from place to place; initially, they could not sell their land without the lord's consent. They could not change jobs or move to another city. Tenants were tied not only to their lord, but to his place.

Women were especially limited; they were bound to a father, a brother, a husband, or a religious order. Just as a man was tied to a lord, a woman was tied to a man with power over her

33

destiny.[9] Rather than citizens of equal status entering contracts with each other, feudal England confronts us as a society in which each person's station in life was set by his or her status— a society defined by lords, commoners, serfs; by bishops, priests, monks; by wives, sisters, daughters, nuns.[10]

What we do not see in this system was widespread "ownership" of property held by persons of equal status who were free to do what they liked with their own land and to sell it, mortgage it, lease it, or give it away on terms chosen by them. In feudal England political and governmental power combined with property rights so that landlords not only controlled their property but governed those on their land. Lords had the power of life and death over the peasants who lived on their land; through control of manorial courts, they had the power to govern those they allowed to live on their land. This power was backed up by the religious sanction of church officials and by the military power of the sword.

Over time, through both political struggles and legal changes, the political power of the lords over the Crown increased; the council of lords became Parliament and King John was forced to sign the Magna Carta. But at the same time, in the field of property law, the power of the lords gradually diminished.[11] With the development of the common law under King Henry II, the royal courts took authority away from the lords' courts and began to protect the property rights of the lords' tenants.[12] Unfreedom gave way to rights and protection from lordly tyranny.

Importantly, over time, the courts began to regulate property rights so as to push power *downward* from the lords to the tenants who lived on the land, making it more and more true that each Englishman was the lord of his own castle. The central royal courts took jurisdiction over all property rights and increasingly protected tenants from arbitrary displacement by the lords. As the peasants gained greater control over their own land, they also gained greater freedom from the lord's whim. Peasants gained both property and freedom not by deregulation; they gained independence by regulatory limitation on the powers of landlords and redistribution of property rights from lords to tenants.

This idea may be hard to accept. Our Lockean tradition is so ingrained that it is quite counterintuitive to believe that freedom came from outlawing certain types of contracts and regulating the rights of owners. But the idea that freedom comes from regulation is easier to understand if we focus on the forms of living we have rejected. Democracy, liberty, and private property, as we conceive them, rest on a rejection of feudalism. Ensuring individuals have the power to determine how to live and what to do with their own property, and granting them the power to buy and sell it, required *taking away the property rights of lords and redistributing those rights to their tenants.* And it required outlawing contracts that tied tenants to lords in a manner that made them servants who must do the lord's bidding, come hell or high water. Conservatives, no less than liberals, enjoy the benefits of the regulatory laws that abolished feudal contracts and property. Conservatives, no less than liberals, should rejoice in the fact that property rights were redistributed from lords to tenants. Conservatives may hate redistribution, but without it we would not have private property; we would have servitude. Conservatives may disparage regulation, but both the freedom and the property rights they cherish came about only because regulation made it so.

Feudalism in America

Nor is this only an English story. Feudalism had an early foothold in America in both New York and New Jersey.[13] In the early 1660s, King Charles II sent Richard Nicolls to invade New York and take it from the Dutch. After successfully accomplishing this, Nicolls followed the King's additional instructions to settle the New Jersey area by giving deeds to several groups of religious dissenters from Massachusetts and Long Island, who settled in the town of Elizabeth in the north and Monmouth County in central New Jersey by the coast. Those deeds gave the settlers title to their lands but also included obligations to pay feudal rents within seven years. The King then gave New Jersey to his brother James, the Duke of York, who promptly assigned it to two men, George Carteret and John Berkeley, to serve as the new Lords Proprietor of the Jerseys. They appointed Carteret's cousin Philip as the first governor of New Jersey. Philip Carteret arrived with a small coterie of soldiers, introduced himself to his new subjects, and let them know that they were now bound to a lord and owed him both fealty and rent.

The New Jersey settlers refused to submit to these lords. They argued that they had been given title to their lands and that they had not been made subject to any lord at that moment. Therefore, they held title to their lands, free of any obligation to a lord. They argued that the King could not take those property rights away once they were granted. It would violate their property rights to impose a lord on them against their will. Some of them also argued that they had title because of deals they made with the Lenni-Lenape Indians who lived in the area. Others argued that they owned their land because they had mixed their labor with the land and built homes and villages. They therefore had three potential sources of title: prior deeds free of any present feudal obligations, treaties with the Indians, and their own labor. They steadfastly held that the claims of the lords to their subservience—and to their rent—could not be imposed on them retroactively against their will.[14]

Obviously, neither Governor Carteret nor Lords Berkeley or Carteret thought this reaction appropriate. Yet the settlers persisted. Not only did they reject the idea that they owed feudal rents to lords they had never agreed to serve, but they claimed the right to govern their own towns. They had title to their land, held it free of rents to any lord, and were capable of governing their own towns themselves. They were equal before God and the King and would not submit to arbitrary taxation or governance by the lords. The lords resisted the claims of the freeholders, and the result was a low-level civil war that lasted more than a hundred years and which ended only a few years before national independence. The heirs of the lords (called the proprietors) continued to seek feudal rents, and the heirs of the freeholders continued to resist by both nonviolent and violent means until the freeholders eventually prevailed.

Feudalism was outlawed in New Jersey, and land ownership was held in a form that is today called a "fee simple"—
property that is inheritable and alienable and free of obligations
to any lord. Ownership of the lands in New Jersey was dispersed
among many owners rather than concentrated in the hands of
two lords, and land was freely bought and sold. After the Revo-
lutionary War, the government was chosen democratically by
these freeholders; office holders were neither appointed by a
monarch nor inherited from a lord. Ownership of public offices
was abolished. One might say every man was lord of his own
castle, but it is more accurate to say that there was no such
thing as a lord anymore. Men were free and equal. Of course,
there were limits to this principle; New Jersey had slavery, and
voting was limited to property owners. Nor did women count as
free and equal persons. But the principle was established, and
principles, once unleashed on the world, have a life of their own.

The capital of Monmouth County is called Freehold and
the county government, to this day, is called the Board of Chosen Freeholders. The freehold movement in New Jersey represents one of the centers where the American conception of
property was born, as well as the American conceptions of both
liberty and democracy.[15]

It was not a foregone conclusion that the United States
would be a democracy. Just as Carteret and Berkeley tried to
establish a feudal regime in New Jersey, Kiliaen van Rensselaer
created a feudal regime in upper New York state at a time when
it was ruled by the Dutch and known as New Netherland.
Granted vast lands along the Hudson River in 1629, van

Rensselaer refused to sell his lands; rather, he created feudal tenancies with personal obligations that included periodic rent payments and other obligations to him as the lord of those lands.[16]

As occurred in New Jersey, those property arrangements led to a long-term struggle between the van Rensselaer heirs and the "tenants" who resisted the obligation to pay rent for the right to occupy land they had already purchased. This struggle was both political and legal, involving electoral politics and lawsuits, and it often skidded into civil disobedience, bringing New Yorkers to the brink of rebellion. Although the courts and legislatures often sided with the proprietors, they sometimes ruled in favor of the tenants.

In the 1852 case of *De Peyster v. Michael*,[17] for example, the New York Court of Appeals ruled that the van Rensselaer heirs could not enforce a "quarter-sale" provision in the deeds. This clause required one-fourth of the sales price of land to be turned over to the heirs of the original lord whenever the land was sold. The court's opinion, written by Chief Judge Charles Ruggles, explained in detail that the people of the state of New York had passed laws to abolish feudalism. A major consequence of that abolition was that lands were freely alienable. Restraints on the transfer of land, such as requirements to obtain the lord's consent to sale, or outright restrictions on transfer, violated the rights of current owners.

The quarter-sale provision was held to be a substantial interference with the alienability of land and thus void. The court explained that "[r]estraints upon alienation of lands held in fee simple were of feudal origin. . . ." Originally, landowners under feudalism could not sell their land without the consent of the lord, and failure to grant such consent would tie the owner to the land—and service to the lord. Chief Judge Ruggles found this social arrangement to be intolerable in a democracy. "This restraint on alienation was a violent and unnatural state of things," he wrote, "contrary to the nature and value of property, and the inherent and universal love of independence."[18] Independence here means not freedom from government regulation, but freedom from control by a lord. Freedom, according to Chief Judge Ruggles, required regulations that take unjust powers away from private owners (the lords) and redistribute those rights to other private owners (the tenants). Freedom required regulation of both contracts and property.

Although the results were less clear in New York than in New Jersey, the legislatures and the courts in both states voiced strong opposition to feudalism as both a political regime and a property system and enacted laws to abolish feudal relationships. It was not always obvious what this meant; landlord-tenant law remained, for example. But it was clear that some contractual arrangements regarding land were out of bounds. In general, it was unlawful to create arrangements that tied tenants to the land and limited their ability to sell or to move. And although landlord-tenant relations have persisted to the present day, American law limits the powers that landlords have over their tenants. Landlords may receive rents from their tenants but they do not rule them. Tenants owe obligations to landlords but they do not serve them. The American abolition of feudalism sought to abolish lordship or to democratize it by making all men lords of their own castles. That is what Ruggles meant when he referred to the American love of independence.

For this reason, over time almost all the states abolished or substantially limited a form of land ownership called the "fee tail." The fee tail gave ownership rights to a person for his lifetime, with title to pass to his heir on his death. The owner of a fee tail could not destroy the interests of the future heirs, whose rights would continue as long as the family line persisted. Only if the line ran out would the property revert to collateral heirs of the original grantor or escheat to the government.[19]

The fee tail contrasted sharply with the fee simple, the most popular form of ownership in the United States. Fee simple rights were fully alienable and inheritable but the heirs had no vested rights to the property. If an owner of fee simple property died without a will, the property would go to the heirs as defined by state law. If the owner left a valid will, the property would go to the persons designated in the will—even if the owner disinherited his children. If the owner sold the property during his lifetime, then the purchaser would step into the place of the seller and the heirs of the seller would have no rights in the land at all. In contrast, if an owner of land held in fee tail sold the property, the buyer would get the property only for the lifetime of the seller; at the seller's death, the property title would immediately go to the seller's heir.[20]

Who would buy such property? For that reason, fee tail property tied up land in the hands of a single family and prevented its free transfer in the marketplace. It encumbered property with residual interests in the heirs of the original owner. Entailed land could not be sold because the buyer's title would automatically end at the death of the seller. That system kept the heir tied to the land. Fee simple property, on the other hand, allowed people to sell their land and to move freely; owners could sell and acquire full title to land. The abolition of the fee tail was part of the American revolt against feudalism and necessary to the creation of modern real estate markets.

How Regulation Abolished Feudalism

Why does this history matter? It matters because it teaches us something of fundamental importance about the nature of property, the free market, and liberty. The limited government championed by conservatives demands the separation of property ownership from political power. Owners control their own property but they do not have the power of life and death over those they allow to come onto their land; they do not govern their tenants or their guests. To have a free society requires a widespread distribution of property (rather than one or two lords), the abolition of unequal statuses, and limitations on the powers of owners over the fate of those they invite onto their land.

This means that we need laws that abolish certain kinds of contracts and property arrangements. If anyone tries to set up a feudal arrangement, the law will not recognize it. In order to create private property and the free market, we need laws that promote widespread distribution of property ownership and we need to prohibit the enforcement of contracts that establish differences of status or which tie people to the land through master-servant relationships. We need to abolish indentured servitude; we need people who are free and independent rather than vassals who pledge loyalty to lords. A free market society bans feudal arrangements.

Notice the implications of this. Because liberals support "regulations" more quickly than do conservatives, it is sometimes thought that they are enemies of "the free market." However, liberals strongly favor the freedoms that markets represent, including freedom from the arbitrary power of a lord and freedom to choose how to live one's life. Conversely, conservatives support more regulation than we may realize. They, as much as liberals, favor a society of free and equal individuals. Conservatives, as much as liberals, want property to change hands in the market, and that requires outlawing contract and property arrangements that unreasonably inhibit the alienability of land. Our regulatory prohibition of feudalism shows that private property and the free market are possible only if we limit freedom of contract and regulate property rights.

Conservatives want small government, free markets, and the protection of property rights, but we can get to the world they value only if we redistribute property rights from lords to commoners, ensure that each person has the opportunity to become an owner, and regulate the terms of contracts and property rights to prevent feudal relationships from being established. Freedom is not possible without regulation, and markets cannot exist without law. The free market is based not on a lack

43

of government regulation but on a regulatory principle that abolishes feudalism and promotes individual choice within the bounds of law.

Conversely, liberals are not in favor of arrangements that tie people to land or to the job that one's father or mother did. They value the freedom to choose where to live and what to do. That requires access to the resources needed to exercise these liberties. For that to happen, there must be equal opportunity to acquire property, and markets must be in place to allow freedom of action and free exchange. Of course, liberals want regulations to ensure that exchange is fair and that property is widespread. But that does not mean they are against markets or private property. Similarly, while conservatives purport to favor free exchange and robust property rights, their commitment to equality of status means that they have no choice but to support laws that ban titles of nobility, feudal privileges, and lordly prerogatives. That means they must favor regulations that ban contractual relationships of this sort, and they should be champions of the redistributions that dethroned lords and enabled peasants to become "lords of their own castles."

The antifeudal principle at the heart of American property and contract law establishes a baseline for market relationships that is enforced through a combination of statutes, common law, and constitutional law. It turns out that the "free market" is not a libertarian idea, and "regulation" is not a liberal idea. Liberals and libertarians alike embrace the regulations necessary to outlaw feudalism and establish the infrastructure for a free and democratic society.

A Society of Free and Equal Persons

Over time, the notion of equality embedded in the antifeudal principle became institutionalized and expanded. It was enshrined in the First Amendment's abolition of any establishment of religion. Property rights are not limited to members of an established church; nor do we make legal distinctions between believers and heretics.[21] The antifeudal principle is evident in the Declaration of Independence's affirmation that "all men are created equal, that they are endowed by their Creator with certain unalienable Rights, that among these are Life, Liberty, and the pursuit of Happiness."[22]

The antifeudal principle was enshrined in the Constitution in 1789 in Article I, Section 9, where the people of the United States ensured that "no Title of Nobility shall be granted by the United States."[23] More than a simple prohibition of Congress giving titles of Duke and Lord, the nobility clause represents the heart of the Constitution, because it evidences the deep break between the egalitarian American system of freehold property and the American system of democracy, and the old, hierarchical, status-based English system of feudalism and monarchy. The states, as well as the federal government, are denied the power to confer titles of nobility and are required by the Constitution to adopt a "republican form of government."[24] That form of government rejects social caste, unequal status, and the power of owners to govern those who enter their land.

The principle of equal status was extended to dramatic effect with the Civil War, the Thirteenth Amendment, and the abolition of slavery. It was extended further in the Married Women's Property Acts of the mid-nineteenth century that freed married women from their prior disabilities and gave them rights to hold and control their own property, to sue and be sued, and to enter enforceable contracts without the consent of their husbands.[25] Those laws partially, but not completely, freed women from the arbitrary power of their husbands.

The principle of equal status was embedded a hundred years later in the civil rights laws of the 1960s, which affirm that access to the marketplace (including public accommodations, employment, and housing) cannot be conditioned on one's race, religion, or sex, and extended in 1988 and 1990 to persons with disabilities.[26] We are currently witnessing the partial expansion of equal status to gay, lesbian, transgender, and bisexual persons. Both the free market and private property exist because we enacted laws that redistributed property rights, regulated the allowable terms of contracts, and prohibited the recognition of unequal statuses based on class, caste, sex, religion, race, or disability, and, increasingly so, sexual orientation.

The Antifeudal Principle in American Property Law

The antifeudal principle is not an archaic relic. It shapes our property law today. For example, it explains why we do not specifically enforce labor contracts. If you want to quit your job, we may force you to pay damages for breach of contract, but courts do not order you to continue working for your employer.[27] If you do not pay your debts, courts may issue orders attaching your wages, but we do not (in general) put you in debtor's prison until you pay off your debts.[28] We do these things not because we do not value liberty or because we are not in favor of "the free market," but because liberty demands the abolition of feudalism and indentured servitude. We regulate the kinds of market relationships and property arrangements that can be established to ensure that we have independent persons free to follow their own paths in their own homes and businesses, subject to legitimate regulations established by law.

We have landlords and tenants, to be sure, but we do not grant landlords the status of lord. Landlords are entitled to get rent from their tenants, but tenants do not owe their landlords service or fealty. Tenants are free to move and to control their own homes.[29] For example, when you rent an apartment, one of the rights you get is the right to invite friends and family over to visit. You do not have to ask your landlord's permission to have guests. In general, the landlord has no power to stop a tenant from receiving visitors; a clause to that effect in a lease is void.[30] Landlords may have powers to exclude persons they believe may be engaging in criminal behavior, and they may prevent tenants from having long-term guests. But such powers are regulated and limited. In a free and democratic society (one that has rejected feudalism), landlords may not isolate their tenants or deprive them of the freedom to exercise the liberties essential to establishing a home.

The New Jersey Supreme Court implemented this principle when it held that a farm owner could not exclude a doctor and a lawyer who wished to visit and provide services to migrant farmworkers living in barracks on his land. Chief Justice Joseph Weintraub explained the basis of this ruling in the abolition of feudalism. "Title to real property cannot include dominion over the destiny of persons the owner permits to come upon the premises."[31] Tenants are neither serfs nor servants, and owners in a free and democratic society have no right to treat them as such. The owner "may not deny the worker his privacy or interfere with his opportunity to live with dignity and to enjoy associations customary among our citizens."[32] Nor may the parties contract to the contrary. "These rights are too fundamental to be denied on the basis of an interest in real property and too fragile to be left to the unequal bargaining strength of the parties."[33] The rights of the tenant to have a home and to receive guests prevail over the freedom of the parties to use the institution of contract to establish property relationships that deny tenants core liberties.

Similar values explain the growth of antidiscrimination law in the mid-twentieth century. Such laws abolished racial segregation mandated by state law, but they also regulated private businesses to ensure equal access to the market without regard to race. Such laws promoted both freedom and equality by regulating the kinds of property rights that could be recognized. Because we tend to conceptualize regulations as deprivations of both freedom and property rights, it was perhaps not surprising that Senator Rand Paul suggested that civil rights laws interfere with the rights of owners. The day after he won the Republican primary for Senate in the state of Kentucky,

Rand Paul did an interview with Rachel Maddow.[34] Although difficult to pin down, he expressed his opinion that the federal public accommodations law of 1964 was problematic and possibly unconstitutional because it interfered with property rights by telling restaurant owners that they could not exclude people from their private property because of race. Paul also suggested that the public accommodations law infringed on free speech rights when it prohibited restaurants from posting "Whites Only" signs.

Senator Paul was fundamentally wrong when he suggested that civil rights laws interfere with property rights and freedom of speech. As a libertarian, he should be aware that liberty cannot exist if some are allowed to rule others. We have abolished both feudalism and slavery. Can private owners exclude others from the market because of their race? If they can, then access to housing, employment, retail stores, and places of entertainment could be conditioned on the color of one's skin. If discriminatory impulses were widespread, then the ability to acquire property would be determined by one's race. Antidiscrimination laws may limit the right to exclude someone from housing, employment, or a public accommodation because of that person's race, but that limitation ensures the ability to acquire property without regard to one's own race. This means not only that the government cannot discriminate on the basis of race but that the private realm of the market cannot distribute property and opportunity on the basis of race.[35] Access to the marketplace cannot be conditioned on race.[36] Your ability to enter the free market will not be limited because of your ancestry or the color of your skin. Free and democratic societies do not recognize social or racial castes and they are not indifferent when private parties try to create such castes. Owners have no right to treat some of their customers as outcasts.

The federal public accommodations law does not interfere with either property rights or liberty because the right to exclude a customer from a restaurant based on race is not a property right that a free and democratic society can recognize. Nor does it infringe on free speech to prohibit an owner from posting a "Whites Only" sign. Allowing restaurants to proclaim their disinclination to serve customers because of race would perpetuate segregated eating establishments and allow racial segregation in the marketplace to persist. Just as we would not recognize feudal relations in America, we do not allow privately created discriminatory barriers to the free market. Such property rights are incompatible with the norms governing a free and democratic society. Because we are not free in a democracy to establish either feudalism or a racial caste society, laws prohibiting those practices do not deprive us of freedom; rather, they promote it. Those laws may limit the freedom of action of racist restaurant owners, but they promote democratic liberty.

While Rand Paul and other libertarians may see the civil rights laws of the 1960s as a regulatory intervention that takes away both property rights and liberty, a direct line can be drawn between these laws and the antifeudal principle at the core of property law. Just as the free market that libertarians identify as a source of freedom demands that property rights not be concentrated among a small group of lords, it also demands that the right to enter the marketplace not be denied to people based on race.

Owners and Neighbors

The antifeudal principle is the source of claims to control one's own property free of intrusive interference by neighbors as well as landlords. Consider that shortly after 9/11, U.S. Supreme Court Justice Clarence Thomas's father-in-law, Donald Lamp, placed an American flag on his condominium balcony.[37] The condominium association asked him to take it down; it had promulgated an aesthetic rule against any decorations such as flags, wind chimes, or banners on the balconies. But Lamp refused to take down his flag. The controversy garnered national attention, and the condominium association backed down. Responding to this kind of dispute, Congress passed a law in 2005 called the Freedom to Display the American Flag Act. That law prohibits enforcement of any condominium covenant or rule that interferes with the ability of any condo owner to fly the American flag.[38]

When this law was being debated, I had two very smart libertarians in my property class. When I asked the students in my class what they thought about the issue, one of the libertarians said that the condo association was in the right. By buying a condominium, Lamp agreed to abide by rules of the association; he simply did not own the right to fly the flag on the balcony. If he wanted to reserve such a right, he should have bought a single-family home. By buying a condominium, he had consented to abide by rules passed by the owners' association and he could not choose which rules to follow and which to ignore. Lamp had exercised his contractual freedom and committed himself to comply with rules passed by the condominium association. The federal statute outlawing the rule would thus interfere with freedom of contract and take property rights away from the neighbors and the association itself.

The other outspoken libertarian in my class became livid. "An American wants to fly the American flag from the balcony of his home after the United States is attacked by foreign enemies and you want the sheriff to come to force him to take it down—and you call yourself a libertarian?" According to this latter view, owners are lords of their own castles in America, and the neighbors have no right to intrude on such fundamental rights of owners. Oppression can come, not just from government officials, but from other private persons, when contract and property arrangements wrongfully give them those powers. We have no lords in America and that means neighbors cannot lord it over you and your property. The federal law, in his view, restored liberty rather than took it away, and it protected the property rights of owners from meddlesome interference by strangers.

My point here is not to establish which position is correct. It is to point out that we cannot decide whether the Freedom to Display the American Flag Act was legitimate by asking whether it constituted a regulatory interference with the free market. Nor should we understand the case to represent a conflict between freedom of contract and property rights. After all, there are property claims on both sides of the dispute; Donald Lamp asserted a right to fly the American flag on his own property, while the neighbors asserted the right to enforce restrictive covenants attached to the owner's rights in the property. While one side argued for the freedom of neighbors to collectively agree to follow rules adopted by the majority (such as limits on the right to fly the flag), the other side argued for the right to be free to use one's property as one sees fit, at least when those rules impinge on fundamental rights like the right to freedom of speech.

Both sides in this dispute want to be free from "lordly power" and to be masters of their own property. The question is what that means in this case. Rather than frame the issue by asking whether we should interfere with the free market or impinge on property rights, we should focus on how to define the appropriate contours for property rights in a free and democratic society. Is the right to fly the American flag from one's home a fundamental right that should be enjoyed by every person? If so, property rights that curtail this right cannot be recognized. That was obviously the opinion of the Congress that passed the law guaranteeing to some the right to fly the American flag. Conservatives championed that law, not because they wanted to interfere with property rights but because they wanted to protect them. They sought not to limit freedom but to promote it. Whether the law was just and fair depends on one's view of the relative rights of flag flyers and their neighbors who seek a uniform external appearance to housing subject to mutual covenants and restrictions. That requires a judgment about the contours of liberty and the plural values we seek to live by. It requires a choice *among* regulations, not a decision *whether or not to regulate.*

The Right to Keep and the Right to Get: Why Democracies Have Many Owners

In addition to limiting the power of some owners over others, the antifeudal principle mandates that there be many owners. A free and democratic society has widely dispersed ownership of property rather than concentrating it in the hands of the few. The subprime crisis brought to our attention the question of how important it is to give all Americans the chance to own their own homes. Those opposed to big government often point to federal policies designed to promote homeownership by low-income families as a major cause of the subprime crisis.[39] Some suggest that our goal of spreading home ownership was a major cause of the problem. The hypothesis does not withstand scrutiny.[40]

Federal regulations adopted after World War II promoted widespread home ownership, and those laws worked well for many years.[41] It was only after the substantial deregulation of the banking sector that the subprime mortgage market emerged.[42] Many nonprofit community development corporations promote housing for low-income families, and these programs face very few defaults.[43] If one wants to promote housing for all Americans, we know how to do this in a manner that works. The subprime market spread ownership in a manner designed to fail. Regulatory laws designed to prevent this from happening again would not only avoid the negative externalities of a subprime market but protect the civil rights of all Americans to fair treatment in the marketplace.

Moreover, while it is true that some people may prefer rental arrangements over ownership, it is important to remember that tenants are subject to disadvantages under existing law relative to owners. For example, tenants can be evicted at the end of the lease term for any nondiscriminatory reason. Only a couple of jurisdictions prohibit eviction without just cause.[44] That means that tenants are far more at the mercy of their landlords than homeowners are of their banks. Rent-paying tenants can be evicted at the end of the lease term at will by the landlord; they therefore have less security in their homes than homeowners do.[45] Responding to the subprime crisis by telling millions of families that they must give up hope that they might participate in the American dream of owning their own homes would make many more people vulnerable to displacement against their will. In that sense, it would undermine the property rights of tenants.

The distribution of homeownership is of crucial importance because concentration of ownership is one of the features of feudalism. Remember the history of New Jersey. A free and democratic society must have more than two owners, and that means the law must redistribute property rights from lords to peasants; Lords Berkeley and Carteret must give way to a community of freeholders. Conservatives, as much as liberals, should endorse redistribution in such a case to promote both liberty and property. Even libertarian hero Robert Nozick acknowledged that someone who comes to own the only water hole in the land is obligated to share the water with others when a drought comes.[46]

Although conservatives and liberals disagree about how much equality we need to have in order to have sufficient opportunity for each person to participate in social and economic life, they do agree on the core principle of equal opportunity and widespread distribution of property.[47] The conservative opposition to "redistribution" is based on the assumption that anyone can become an owner in our society by working hard and following the rules. But that assumption is justified only if property is sufficiently widely distributed—and well-paying jobs are widely available. As a matter of principle, it is clear that conservatives value dispersed ownership as much as do liberals. They do so because it is the mark of a democratic society that has abolished titles of nobility.

Democratic Liberty

A democratic society recognizes each person as free and equal. Such societies do not emerge from a state of nature. They are born from struggles to limit the power of kings and lords and to free slaves and servants from their masters. History teaches us that this can be achieved only by regulating the terms of contractual and property arrangements to abolish feudal and slave relationships and to spread access to property and opportunity. The world that both conservatives and liberals envision is one of many owners, with equal status, each free to pursue her dreams and control her own life. Such a world is possible only if ownership of property is widespread, people are not legally bound to serve others, and people are not denied access to markets because of their race or sex or other characteristics that might cast them in a subordinate, unequal role. Far from regulation-free zones, both markets and property are constituted by laws designed to ensure both liberty and equality.

3

Why Consumer Protection Promotes the Free Market

It was easier to make a revolution than to write 600 to 800
laws to create a market economy.

—JIRI DIENSTBIER

I n 2010, Congress created a new federal agency designed to
regulate consumer credit to prevent some of the worst
excesses of the subprime crisis from happening again.
Yet shortly after President Obama's second inauguration,
the Republicans in Congress were doing what they could to restructure the Consumer Financial Protection Bureau (CFPB) in a
manner that would make it more difficult for it to do its job.
They voiced their objections in procedural and institutional
terms, arguing that the agency head had too much power and
that the agency was not subject to sufficient checks and balances—especially congressional oversight.[1] The Democrats believed all this to be a ruse, that the agency was already subject
to sufficient checks and balances, and that what Republicans
really abhorred was the attempt to regulate consumer financial
markets at all.[2]

Whatever the truth of the matter, it is revealing that even those Republicans who were seeking to restructure the agency claimed to be "supporters of strong and effective consumer protections."[3] Republicans want limited government and oppose government regulation. Consumer protection laws regulate the way products and services are offered as well as their substantive features. Given their professed aversion to "regulation," one might think that Republicans would really like to free financial markets entirely from the regulations passed since the subprime crisis. But they nonetheless profess support for "strong and effective" consumer protection law. Why is that?

They do so partly because all of us learned painful lessons from the subprime crisis. We learned that people can be fooled into taking on financial burdens that they cannot bear and that these arrangements have the potential to undermine economic prosperity for all of us. We learned that when we begin to gamble on the infrastructure of economic life, we pose undue risks to ourselves and our neighbors. And we learned that markets will better reflect our preferences if we enact laws that ensure that we get what we bargain for.

Far from interfering in the free market or undermining economic efficiency, consumer protection law is a cornerstone of well-functioning markets. It promotes freedom of contract and social welfare and it protects property rights. Not only do free markets work better if we have consumer protection law, but it turns out that, without such laws, they cannot work at all. Whether you know it or not, if you are a champion of free markets, then you are also a champion of consumer protection laws.

Once again, we will see that regulation (sensible regulation) promotes markets rather than undermines them.

How Consumer Protection Laws Help Us Get What We Want

Every state has a consumer protection statute. That is true even of the most libertarian of our states. This is surprising. From a libertarian perspective, such laws might well be understood as inimical to freedom because they regulate the content of contractual relationships. We typically associate freedom of contract norms with the liberty to choose the terms of your contracts. If you want something, bargain for it. This approach might suggest a policy of caveat emptor—let the buyer beware. Laws that mandate the substantive terms of contracts arguably limit our choices; they prevent us from making bargains that are prohibited by those laws. For that reason, Alan Schwartz has argued that mandatory terms regulations prevent people from "do[ing] the best they can for themselves, given their circumstances."[4] People want freedom of action, and regulatory laws limit our freedom. Why, then, does every state have consumer protection laws? Why adopt laws that deprive us of choices? Why do even conservative states have these laws?

The reason we have consumer protection laws is that people want them. And people want them not because they limit our freedom, but because *they help us get what we want*. They do this by freeing us from unfair or deceptive practices.[5] Every state has a consumer protection statute that prohibits such business practices.[6] And the Federal Trade Commission Act similarly prohibits "unfair or deceptive acts or practices in or affecting commerce."[7] We want protective laws not because we are uninterested in freedom and not because we are uninterested in the liberty to determine the terms of our contracts. We want consumer protection laws because we want to be free from worrying about bad things happening to us. One of the bad things that can happen to us is being surprised by the terms of a contract we enter. We also fear products that do not operate as promised, that will harm us rather than help us. We want to know that when we go into the market to buy goods or services, we will get what we want rather than be cheated or placed in danger. We want to be able to stop worrying about things we should not have to fear. We want to know that the products and services we buy are safe and will work as advertised. Consumer protection laws do not take away our freedom; they enable us to exercise it. They do not prevent us from doing what we want to do; they help us to get what we want.

Caveat emptor forces us to treat every potential contracting party as an enemy who cares not a whit about our welfare. It makes us presume that we cannot trust them, that they are out to get whatever they can from us. In contract negotiations, if law gave us no protection, we would have to remember to ask for everything we want, and that can be a long list. Think of a tenant renting an apartment in Boston. She wants working heating facilities, hot water, a shower, bathrooms, plumbing that works, windows that are not broken and that open and close. She wants the apartment to be free of pests. She wants to be free from sexual harassment by the landlord. She wants the other tenants to have an obligation not to disturb her quiet enjoyment. She wants to be able to get married and have her spouse move in with her. She wants . . . etc.

If you cannot assume that a transaction gets you what you want, you have to remember to ask for every single little thing that goes along with a transaction of that sort. You have to enter the store with a long list of things to ask for. This is exhausting and anxiety-producing. We want to be able to trust the businesses we contract with, and consumer protection laws enable us to do that by ensuring that we get what most people would want if they entered a transaction of that sort.

We want to get a package of entitlements when we enter typical contractual relationships; another word for such packages is "property." Property rights generally comprise a bundle of rights that is standardized but customizable. When we buy a house, we will have the right to live in it, exclude others, invite friends for dinner, mortgage it, sell it, leave it to our children, etc. Any limitations on the standard package must be negotiated. The same is true for other consumer transactions. We want the arrangement to reflect our justified expectations. Consumer protection laws try to ensure this to be the case.

What we want is freedom from fear. We want the freedom for things to go as we wish they would. Hobbes argued that we created government because the state of nature was dangerous and we were vulnerable to violent death by being attacked by others trying to take our stuff. Laws against murder and assault and battery free us to walk the streets without fear. So too do consumer protection laws allow us to focus less on protecting ourselves from monsters and more on having fun.

Consider building codes that regulate housing construction. These laws require housing to be built in a safe manner out of safe materials by competent, licensed builders who have demonstrated that they know what they are doing. They ensure that buildings are accessible to people with disabilities and that they are sufficiently durable and protected against the threats of earthquakes, fires, floods, and lead paint. These laws are enforced by housing inspectors who issue building permits and who visit construction sites to make sure that construction complies with regulatory requirements. These rules interact with zoning laws that limit the size of buildings and create setback requirements and which segregate different property uses into different zones of the municipality. Building codes and zoning laws limit our freedom to build buildings that do not comply with those regulations. By definition, they increase the costs of housing. At the same time, they save money by preventing injury.

A libertarian might focus on the fact that building codes and zoning laws limit freedom of contract. Such laws prevent us from hiring unlicensed contractors or doing the work ourselves. They try to stop us from using substandard materials or building structures that fail to meet certain minimum standards. They prevent us from building a store in the middle of a residential neighborhood even if that is the most valuable use of the property. These laws limit our choices and thereby inhibit our freedom to deviate from centrally mandated norms. Standard packages of rights are one thing; laws that make those rights nonwaivable are another thing entirely; they remove our freedom to enter into contracts that do not reflect the terms mandated by government. They interfere with freedom of action. Why, then, does every state not only protect consumers but make such protection nondisclaimable?

There are three basic answers to this question. The first concerns externalities—effects on others who are not party to our contracts. An unsafe house imposes vulnerabilities or costs on others. If the electrical wiring is done incorrectly, the house can burn down. And a burning house represents a danger not just to those inside, but to the neighbors. And such costs are borne not just by neighbors but by the taxpayers who fund firefighting services. The danger to neighbors is significant. Believe me when I say this is not a trivial problem. My brother's house burned down because the prior owner decided to do his own electrical work and didn't know what he was doing. If it had been a windy day ... Well, let's just say the neighbors called 911, not just as a service to my brother who was not at home at the time, but to protect their own property and lives.

A second answer is that mandatory terms in laws like building codes help people get what they want. Why is that? How can a law that limits contractual choice help us get what we want? Why don't people just bargain for the level of building safety and quality that they prefer? Why mandate a "one size fits all" regulation? The answer is that minimum standards regulations do a better job of helping us get what we want than do regulations that merely create default terms that we may bargain away.

Recall that consumer protection laws help us get what we want by ensuring that the contract reflects the justified expectations of the consumer. Caveat emptor requires the buyer to remember and bargain for all the details of the transaction; consumer protection laws save the consumer the cost and trouble of doing that and protect us from the vulnerabilities we would face if we forgot to bargain for something. If consumer protection laws merely created default terms—terms that we were free to bargain away—then sellers would have an incentive to do just that. They would write long contracts (like those long technical agreements we all click on when we buy things on the Internet). Those contracts would likely serve the interests of sellers by getting consumers to waive all those protections provided by consumer protection statutes—and we would be right back where we started. We would have to read the contracts carefully, hire a lawyer if we did not understand the technical language, and bargain for the specific terms we want.

Consumers have neither the time nor the inclination to do all this. Nor can they afford the legal services that would be necessary to help them understand and bargain for appropriate contract terms. Mandatory terms regulations ensure that the contracts say what most people would want them to say. They ensure that we get what we want. Waivable terms would not achieve the same result.

Consumer protection laws do not take away our freedom; they give us the freedom to take certain things for granted. *There are some things that we should not have to bargain for.* When we buy a house, we want to be free to assume that it is safe and that it provides certain basic amenities. We do not want to have to waste time trying to figure out the long list of things we expect to get when we buy a house. We want a standard package of minimum requirements that we can assume will be there. We want to be freed from the obligation to have to bargain about all these basic things. We want to be free to bargain about other things. Minimum standards regulations do not prevent us from bargaining to obtain additional protections or amenities. They free us from having to bargain for the things almost all of us want.

Of course, this may deprive some of the freedom to enter an arrangement that does not comply with minimum standards. But giving that person the freedom to enter such a contract harms the rest of us by depriving us of the freedom to get what we want when we buy a house. "Deregulating" building construction would indeed promote greater "freedom of contract" in the sense that limits on contractual terms would be absent. But it would deprive most of us of the liberty of knowing that we will get what most people would want if they entered a transaction of this sort. Removing building codes does not promote freedom; it allows those who do not care about safe homes to impose their will on the rest of us. Of course, we could still bargain for the terms we want; but that brings us back to the problem that we are unlikely to remember or even know what all those terms are. That is why we want state laws that adopt regulations created by building experts to ensure that homes are safe and habitable and not a danger to the neighbors. That is why we want regulatory laws that create minimum standards regulations for consumer transactions.

Should consumer protection laws make consumer protections disclaimable? Either way, someone will be imposing their preferences on someone else. Minimum standards regulations do inhibit the freedom of action of those who want to bargain for lesser protections. But "deregulation" would solve their problem only at the cost of subjecting the rest of us to the uncertainty associated with not having minimum standards requirements. The loss in freedom of action for some provides liberty for others.

We have a right to get what we pay for. We have a right not to be cheated. Not only do we want to be free from the need to figure out and remember the long list of things we are trying to get out of a complex deal, we want to be free from worry that we are being asked to endure conditions that we should not have to bear. A house in Boston is not a house if it does not have heating facilities. Beyond the fact that we do not want to have to bargain to make sure there is a working furnace in the house, we have a right not to be subjected to a house that lacks heat and hot water. We want to be free from fear of conditions we should not have to bear. People lobby for and support consumer protection laws not because they are indifferent to freedom, but because they want freedom. They want to be free to assume that goods and services comply with reasonable minimum standards that most people expect and desire. Consumer protection laws do not limit our freedom; they promote our freedom by helping us get what we want.

The American Demand for Law

Americans tend to talk like "small-government" libertarians, but we legislate like liberals. Our prevailing rhetoric decries intrusive regulation, but *Americans have a prodigious demand for law*. We have seen why some types of property and contract rights must be banned in societies that protect individual rights and that treat each person as equal and free. Social and economic relationships in a free and democratic society are subject to minimum standards regulations designed to protect the dignity and liberty of each person. But our laws not only prohibit feudalism and slavery, they establish minimum standards to ensure that when we enter the marketplace we are protected from being harmed or cheated and that the products and services we buy will comply with certain basic standards.

Minimum standards regulations exist not because we do not value freedom, but precisely because we do value it. Such laws represent collective political choices about the basic protections we have the right to expect when we enter market transactions. They define the contexts within which we exercise our liberties. We want not only the freedom to choose our contract terms, but the freedom to decide collectively through political processes the environment within which we live. Collective choices about context are the way a free and democratic society uses law to define and promote the liberties to which free and equal persons are entitled.

Minimum standards regulations promote both conservative and liberal values. While laws seem to limit our freedom, they also enhance it in ways that libertarians have long understood. Consider legal protections against fraud. Conservatives who condemn "government regulation of the free market" generally support laws that protect people from fraud. Why? Because fraud is a kind of theft. Taking money under false pretenses is the opposite of a free and voluntary agreement; it is a wrongful deprivation of property rights. And conservatives are champions of the rights of property owners. Consumer protection laws protect us from deceptive practices and, in so doing, reflect libertarian values. Freedom of contract means the freedom to enter a contract and the freedom not to enter a contract. We are free to commit ourselves to obligations to others only as long as we can trust that the deal will reflect our actual expectations and desires. Fraudulent business practices undermine our ability to enter contracts that reflect our preferences.

Minimum standards regulations promote "freedom of contract" not only by protecting us from fraud and deception but by protecting our property rights. Some conservatives rail against some environmental laws because they prevent owners from developing their property and because they increase the cost of goods and services. But such laws do more than just limit what we can do with our property. They protect our property from incompatible neighboring uses; they protect our property and our communities from devastation and destruction. While conservatives may lobby against particular regulations, they generally do not oppose them entirely. Many conservatives favor zoning law and environmental law even though those regulations limit what we can do with our own property.

Zoning laws protect our property rights by ensuring that our property has a certain character. When you buy a single-family house, you may want not just the house and the land but a house in a neighborhood with other single-family homes. You want some security in knowing that the environment in which your house is situated is of a certain character. We achieve this result through zoning law and through covenants in real estate deeds that create homeowners' associations with powers to create and enforce rules about the use of property in the neighborhood. Such laws limit our property so that we can be assured that our neighbors are similarly limited. For many people those regulations enhance the value and utility of property rather than undermine it.

Similarly, although conservatives oppose particular environmental regulations, they do not lobby to repeal the Clean Air Act or the Clean Water Act. They value protecting their children from pollution as strongly as do liberals. We may want the freedom to use our property as we wish, but we do not have the right to use our property in ways that pollute the property of our neighbors or that destroy shared resources in water and air. Conservatives are not actually against environmental law; they simply oppose environmental laws they deem to be unnecessary. If we look at what they do rather than what they say, it is apparent that many conservatives support a lot more regulation in these areas than one might think.

On April 5, 2010, an explosion at a coal mine owned by Massey Energy Company killed twenty-nine miners. While it is still unclear what caused the explosion, the Upper Big Branch

Mine had been cited repeatedly for safety violations, and both federal mining officials and the company had been concerned about safety at the mine.[8] Efforts to alleviate unsafe workplace conditions have been a staple of government regulation for a long time—not to mention the stuff of novels and popular movies. Charles Dickens and Upton Sinclair come to mind.[9] It is apparent that the profit motive sometimes is stronger than the moral impetus to ensure the safety and well-being of workers. For this reason, both the federal government and the state governments have passed comprehensive laws designed to regulate the workplace environment to increase, if not ensure, the safety of workers.

I have argued that we are a country that prizes freedom and is skeptical of government regulation. Yet I do not recall hearing anyone say that those men would be alive today if only we had less government regulation of mines. The general reaction was one of horror and sympathy for the families and a desire to find out what went wrong and whether it could be prevented in the future. There were musings about how dangerous coal mining is and how heroic the miners are to provide energy resources that many of us depend on. And there were widespread questions about whether existing regulations were strong enough.

While many Americans voice skepticism about government in general and say they want a smaller government, they tend to respond to social problems by seeking government regulations. We are opposed to regulation in general but strongly supportive of it in particular. Along with our allergic reaction to the idea of government regulation is our insistent demand for laws to protect us from unfair treatment, unsafe conditions, and harmful conduct.

Americans have different conceptions of both "liberty" and "the free market" than the ones trumpeted by libertarians. Americans seek not only the freedom to deal on mutually chosen terms, but the freedom from being cheated or treated badly.[10] We seek safety when we enter the marketplace; we seek products that work as promised and that will not injure us.[11] We seek safe workplaces.[12] We want insurance companies to have enough money to pay valid claims when due and to ensure that they actually do pay those claims rather than delay in bad faith.[13] We want our bank accounts protected.[14] We want our buildings to be safe and our electricians to be licensed so that our houses do not burn down because of incompetent contractors.[15] We want marriages regulated so that we are not left destitute following divorce or the death of a spouse.[16] We want land use regulated by zoning and environmental laws so that we have clean water and air and can live in a suitable environment.[17] We want access to the marketplace without regard to race, sex, religion, or disability.[18]

Laws like this exist in every state—including those one might consider to be the most libertarian in orientation.[19] We want freedom of choice in the marketplace but we also want to choose the contexts within which those choices are made. Regulatory laws that set minimum standards for market relations provide that for us. Americans may have a fierce libertarian streak but Americans also demand law—and a lot of it. We want to shape the environment within which we exercise our freedom. That's why we demand regulation. We use political processes to choose representatives who pass laws we want. We exercise choice, not only in the marketplace, but in the political sphere as well.

We want law not because we want protection from our own stupidity or irrationality, and not because we do not care about liberty. We demand law because we want to take certain things for granted. When we enter a retail store, we want to know that we can leave; the store owner is not our lord and has no dominion over us just because we are on his land. He cannot detain us without cause (such as a reasonable belief we were stealing his goods). When we buy a product, we want to know it will act as advertised and be safe. When we buy services, we want our providers to know what they are doing. When sellers get us to buy things, we want to know that we are not being taken for a ride or treated differently because of our race. Regulatory laws free us from having to bargain about all these things every time we enter the market, leaving us free to bargain about other things.

Consumer protection laws that set minimum standards for market relationships do not take away our freedom or interfere with the free market. Rather, they ensure that we get what we want in the marketplace. While it is true that laws that establish mandatory terms for contracts may deprive some of the ability to contract for different terms, consumer protection laws ensure that market transactions accord with the legitimate expectations of most persons. Such laws not only save us from the transaction costs of having to bargain for basic protections but represent a politically adopted framework for fair market relationships. Mandatory rules are sometimes based on court interpretation of constitutional provisions and sometimes on court interpretation of the common law; at other times, they are defined by statutes or administrative rules. We use a variety of lawmaking procedures to engage in collective choices about the minimum standards we want for governing economic relationships. Such laws allow us to take many things for granted by freeing us from the need to have to bargain about basic protections when we enter the marketplace. If we look at what we do, rather than at what we say, it is apparent that Americans are fiercely supportive of government regulation—not because we do not value freedom but because we do value it.

Why Regulations Don't Hurt the Poor

Arguments for "regulation" face an inevitable critique: don't they increase the cost of providing goods and services, hurting all consumers and especially the poor? This argument is worth considering, but when someone makes it you should hang on to your wallet. The question suggests that all regulations backfire by hurting those they are meant to protect. The problem is that the argument proves too much. If it were true, it would mean that we should deregulate entirely. I have explained why this would be impossible; it would be contrary to the idea of having a free market and private property in the first place. But the argument is equally wrong if we focus on the claim that new regulations (added to those we already have) increase the cost of providing goods and services and thus inevitably hurt those they were intended to protect.[20] Here is why.

It is true that the cost of housing would probably be cheaper if we repealed building codes. Some providers would try to sell shoddy housing and it is likely some buyers with high tolerance for risk would purchase such housing in order to save money. But the lack of regulation would mean that we could not be sure that our homes were safe. We want building codes because they ensure (or make it more likely) that when we buy a house we will not be moving into a firetrap or face injury from a collapsing stairwell. We want freedom from the need to bargain about these things when we buy a home; we want to take it for granted that the building was constructed according to certain minimum standards. Of course, such regulations make housing more expensive, but to most citizens (those who supported passage of building code laws) the benefits of these regulations outweigh the costs.[21]

It is an elementary mistake in logic to assume that a regulation is bad because it imposes costs. If that were true, we would never buy anything. Of course rules impose costs; the question is whether the benefits are greater than the costs. Conversely, it is illogical to assume we would suffer no costs if we got rid of minimum standards regulations. In fact, we would suffer costs galore. If we are judging regulations by whether they promote our interests, we must attend to not only the costs they impose but their benefits; and we must compare their net benefits (or costs) with the net benefits or costs of not having a particular regulation.

It is true that building code legislation may have the effect of pricing the poorest Americans out of the housing market. They could afford housing if it were legal to sell a shack. But the way to help the poor is not to make housing unsafe for the rest of us. The way to help the poor is to increase their incomes so that they can afford minimally decent housing. This can be done in many ways—by giving the poor subsidies or by increasing their access to well-paying jobs or by ensuring affordable, safe child care. If our laws have not made it possible for individuals to earn enough for a living, that is the fault not of those individuals, but of our laws. A democracy values each person equally; we each have the right to pursue happiness. That means that property must be distributed and regulated so that each person can participate in our markets. To demand that we remove regulations that protect all of us to make products affordable by the poorest persons is to make the tail wag the dog. We want regulations that set minimum standards for market and property relationships, and we help the poor, not by making the rest of us vulnerable to unsafe housing, but by enabling the poor to raise their incomes or to obtain needed services in other ways.

The argument that regulations inevitably hurt the poor is an argument that proves too much. If we follow its implications to the end, it would require us to deny ourselves the benefits of laws that help us get what we want when we enter the marketplace. It also is a perverse interpretation of what it means to give the poor what they want. "Deregulation" may make housing affordable for the poor, but it would be lousy housing. The poor do not want lousy housing. They agree to live in it only because they do not have the market power to insist on housing that is minimally decent. It is the job of law to ensure that the housing they obtain does comply with minimum standards compatible with human dignity. If the price of such housing is too high relative to the incomes of the poor so that they cannot afford it, then we must figure out how to provide such housing to the poor. At least, that is the case if we believe the proposition that "all [persons] are created equal" and that all, including the poor, have the right to "life, liberty, and the pursuit of happiness."

Why Subprime Mortgages Were Deceptive

The subprime crisis has made us painfully aware of the reasons for consumer protection law. Not only did such mortgages result in disaster for many families; they wrecked the world economy and created hardship for many people. Consumer protection laws prohibit unfair and deceptive practices. Let's first discuss why subprime mortgages were deceptive and then focus on why they were unfair.

Laws promoting disclosure and preventing deceptive practices should be embraced by conservatives and liberals alike. Deceptive practices induce people to enter into agreements they would not make if they had adequate information. They are a species of fraud and the opposite of the principle of freedom of contract. We are free to make contracts with others, but we are also free not to make contracts. Agreements make both parties better off than they were before the agreement because each is getting something it wants and giving up something it is willing to exchange for what it gets. Deception in the contracting process induces agreements that are not in the best interests of both parties. Both fraud (lying about a material fact to induce agreement) and deception (making misleading statements or failing to reveal information the other side would want to know) undermine any sense that contract enforcement promotes the will or the interests of both parties. It is akin to diverting someone's attention so you can pick that person's pocket. For that reason, deception is a form of theft. It not only contravenes freedom of contract norms but violates the property rights of the victim.

There was a lot of deception in the subprime mortgage market. Borrowers were often misled about the interest rates they would be paying. It was common for even knowledgeable borrowers to be surprised by sudden rises in mortgage payments. This happened because the mortgage documents were so complicated and because the mortgage brokers failed to explain clearly what the borrowers were getting into. If the borrowers had readily understood what the real interest rate was, some would not have agreed to the loan at all.

Federal Reserve Board Governor Ned Gramlich noted, "Why are the most risky loan products sold to the least sophisticated borrowers? The question answers itself. The least sophisticated borrowers are probably duped into taking these products."[22] Mortgage brokers who did explain the intricacies of adjustable rate mortgages assured borrowers that they could refinance when the interest rates increased. They did not explain, however, that this ability to refinance would disappear if housing prices stalled or plummeted. They induced borrowers to ignore such real concerns. Similarly, banks misled investors in securitized mortgages by giving AAA ratings to subprime mortgages held by people who could not afford to pay them back if housing prices decreased.

Subprime mortgage marketing rested on mixed messages. Subprime borrowers were told that they had to pay high interest rates because they posed a high credit risk, but they were then told they would never have to pay those high, unaffordable rates because they could refinance. They were not told or did not understand that this would work only if property values continued to rise for the entire term of their mortgage—a highly risky proposition when repayment occurs over twenty or thirty years. Similarly, investors in mortgage-backed securities were told that they paid high returns because subprime loans were so risky, but then the bankers arranged for the securities to have AAA ratings, suggesting that they posed no risk at all. High return, low risk. This message is too good to be true, and it turned out that it was too good to be true. What the consumers and investors relied on was the bankers' assurances that the loans were suited to subprime borrowers and safe for risk-averse investors. The banks took advantage of mixed messages because they knew that their customers would trust them. Mixed messages are deceptive because they are designed to induce people to hear the bad news and then ignore it. They are designed to promote trust while violating it.

We could of course debate how much deception there was or what forms of market practice are acceptable. One could argue that borrowers and investors made free choices to invest in risky purchases, that they made high returns for taking those risks, and that the downside is a risk they voluntarily took on themselves. If all this is true, borrowers and investors have no one to blame but themselves for their misfortune. They assumed the risk, and we have no good reason to depart from the traditional doctrine of caveat emptor. This argument has merit for some consumers and for some transactions, but it does require distinguishing between acceptable and unacceptable business practices. The law prohibits not only outright fraud, but also deceptive practices. The federal securities laws that protect shareholders who invest in stocks prohibit not only misleading statements but omissions that convey a false impression about facts investors would want to know in deciding whether to invest in a company's stock.[23] One could argue for repealing state consumer protection laws and federal trade and securities regulation, but the truth is that both consumers and sophisticated investors want protection from deceptive practices. These laws do not interfere with freedom of contact; rather they ensure that people get what they want when they buy or invest.[24] In so doing, they also protect private property by ensuring that businesses cannot take your money on false or misleading pretenses.

Better and clearer information might have avoided some of the problem. The new Consumer Financial Protection Bureau (CFPB) is issuing regulations designed to improve disclosure.

These rules not only will give better guidance to the banks on what they have to disclose but will help consumers better understand the terms of the mortgages they are taking on.

Why Subprime Mortgages Were Unfair

Consumer protection laws prohibit unfair transactions. Subprime mortgages were unfair as well as deceptive. They were unfair both to the borrowers themselves and to the third parties who suffered their ill effects. They were unfair to others because they were unaffordable to the borrowers once interest rates adjusted from initial low rates to the higher rates. When that happened, foreclosures resulted in the millions. That in turn affected the investors who had bought subprime mortgage-backed securities and the rest of us who have suffered through an economic recession as a result. It also hurt the communities who have been decimated by foreclosures and by the failures of banks to maintain foreclosed properties.

It may be true that subprime mortgages were unfair to the rest of us by causing us hardship. But how were subprime mortgages unfair to the borrowers themselves? After all, didn't the borrowers agree to these mortgages? Didn't they want them? Wouldn't it be unfair to prevent them from becoming home-owners by outlawing subprime mortgages? If we ban subprime mortgages aren't we depriving people of the chance to borrow money and become homeowners? Doesn't that sacrifice their freedom for the good of the community? Doesn't that violate their rights rather than promote fairness and justice?

It is true that regulations that ban or discourage high interest loans to those who do not qualify for prime loans limit their freedom to enter such transactions. But this is no more unfair to people with poor credit ratings than building code regulations and zoning laws are unfair to them. Those regulatory laws protect everyone, including low-income persons, from market arrangements likely to bring them to financial ruin. There are ways to help low- and moderate-income families obtain housing. Subprime mortgages are not one of them.

What was it about them that was inherently unfair? The Supreme Judicial Court of the Commonwealth of Massachusetts explained that it is unfair to grant a mortgage to a borrower who cannot pay it back.[25] One such scenario occurs when the loan is structured so as to make refinancing impossible if housing values fall. Consider how subprime mortgages work. Rather than rent housing, the subprime borrower takes out a loan with a very high interest rate in order to purchase a home. To make the loan immediately affordable, the bank gives the borrower an initial teaser rate that is very low. Because the borrower has a low income or a poor credit rating, the bank charges an above-prime interest rate after the initial teaser period. That rate increases monthly payments to such a high level that the borrower is very likely to default. In such a case, unless the borrower can refinance (get a new loan) at an affordable rate, the buyer will lose the house. Because the post-teaser-rate monthly mortgage payments are likely to be higher than average monthly rental payments, the borrower will be worse off than if that person had never bought the house but had simply rented all along.

It is not better to have owned and lost than never to have owned at all.

The borrower can avoid default only by refinancing when the interest rate rises. But that can happen only if property values keep rising. If they fall, the value of the property may be less than the outstanding loan. Such a house is "underwater," and no bank will loan $200,000 to someone who possesses a house worth only $100,000; there is not enough collateral to ensure repayment of the loan. Refinancing is impossible and so foreclosure is inevitable unless the bank chooses, for its own economic reasons, to delay foreclosure.

The same result may happen when the mortgage agreement provides for a stiff prepayment penalty. If refinancing can happen only if the borrower pays a prepayment penalty up front, and the borrower does not have the money to make that payment, then the borrower cannot refinance; nor can the borrower borrow more money to make that payment if the market value of the house has decreased, leaving the borrower no collateral to support a second loan. The same is true if the borrower has no equity in the property because the person borrowed 100 percent of the purchase price, and so even a slight drop in property values would mean the outstanding loan is likely to be higher than the market value of the property. Again, the bank will not refinance if the loan is backed by property worth less than the loan.

Some borrowers were willing to take these risks. Others were deceived into taking them. It was perhaps not unfair to give subprime mortgages to those who fully understood the risks and voluntarily embraced them. But that was not true about most subprime borrowers. They took out these mortgages not because they hoped to flip houses and benefit from rising property values; they took out mortgages because they wanted a home. They wanted to share in the American dream. The banks that created and marketed subprime mortgages did not really help people do that. They created the illusion that they were helping people buy homes. In reality, when property values stalled or decreased, millions of people would be stripped of their homes, and because so many houses were underwater, the homeowners would also be stripped of their equity. And they would have been paying more money than if they had rented rather than bought. So they would lose not only their homes but the money in their bank accounts they otherwise could have retained and used for other purposes.

Subprime mortgages were unfair because they were, as Senator Elizabeth Warren has explained, the moral equivalent of exploding toasters. When we enter the marketplace to buy a car, we rely on the expertise of the car company—and consumer protection law—to create a car that is safe. When we hire a doctor, we rely on licensing requirements to ensure the doctor is knowledgeable and trained. Most of us do not have the expertise to judge whether goods and services providers are doing a good job. We rely on providers of goods to treat us fairly by selling us safe products that work, and we rely on service providers to treat us fairly by providing competent services. We trust them, or we want to be able to trust them.

Borrowers who took on subprime mortgages trusted the banks that induced them to take out these loans. They assumed the bank would not loan them money that they could not pay back. They believed the mortgage brokers when they said the borrower could refinance and would never have to pay the unaffordable high interest rate. Banks have an obligation to respect the justified expectations of their customers. Granting a loan the bank knows the borrower is highly likely to regret is the moral equivalent of selling a dangerous product. Consumer protection laws are designed precisely to protect us from being taken advantage of in this way. If you would not sell a defective car to your mother, you should not sell it to someone else's mother.

Consumers are not making a mistake when they trust businesses to treat them fairly. They are entitled to believe that businesses like banks know what they are doing and that the products they sell will operate as advertised. Customers who trust bankers are doing nothing wrong. Banks that take advantage of mixed messages or that sell products designed to impoverish the customer are not engaged in free commerce; they are manipulating consumers to strip them of their wealth. We have consumer protection laws not because people are stupid or foolish; we have such laws because pressures to pursue profits can induce businesses to sell what they should not sell. In such cases, it is the sellers, not the buyers, who are morally responsible for unfair outcomes. We do not, after all, blame people when thieves pick their pockets; we do not say "Shame on you for carrying money around on your person." No, we blame the thief.

It is apparent that we need laws preventing banks from selling mortgages to people who cannot afford them, to protect both those families from harm and the rest of us from the externalities of subprime mortgages. Once again, the Consumer Financial Protection Bureau (CFPB) adopted rules designed to achieve this goal. Final regulations have now been issued to prevent granting high-priced mortgages to those who cannot afford them and to provide presumptive protection for "qualified mortgages" that meet certain affordability criteria.[26] Those rules seek to limit mortgage payments to 41 percent of one's monthly income to ensure that borrowers can afford to make those payments. The goal is to prevent banks from saddling borrowers with onerous monthly payments that are very likely to lead to default and foreclosure. It is both unfair and unwise to loan someone money if the person cannot pay it back. And loaning the money on the supposition that property values will rise forever is unreasonable, as we have now found out.

Both libertarians and many economists criticize laws that regulate the terms of mortgages because they increase the costs of borrowing and may make it impossible for low- and moderate-income families to buy a home. I have explained that this argument, taken to the extreme, would counsel abolishing all regulatory laws, including building codes, zoning laws, and environmental laws. It would also suggest going back to strict foreclosure, an illegal process that enables banks to foreclose and keep the full value of the property rather than giving the borrower time to repay the loan and allowing the person to keep any equity she built up in the house.

For example, suppose you borrow $200,000 to purchase a $250,000 home. You make payments for ten years, by which time you have paid $100,000 of your $200,000 debt. Then you lose your job and default on your mortgage payments. Assume the market value of the property has now risen to $400,000. Under a system of strict foreclosure, your default allows the bank to kick you out and take possession of the house. That means that the bank gets a house worth $400,000 to ensure it gets the rest of its loan back. But only $100,000 remains on the loan. If the bank can keep the house, it gets not only its $100,000 back but $300,000 more. The mortgage laws of every state prevent this result by regulating foreclosure; those laws seek to induce a foreclosure sale at fair market value, which gives both the bank its money back and the borrower/homeowner the right to the "equity" in the home— that is, the excess of the foreclosure sale price above that needed to pay off the rest of the debt. Under foreclosure laws, if they operate properly, the home would be sold because of the home-owner's default. It would garner $400,000 (the current fair market value of the property). The bank would get the rest of its loan back ($100,000 plus interest and costs), and the homeowner would get the rest ($300,000 minus interest and costs).

Every state has mortgage laws regulating foreclosure to protect the interests of both the lending bank and the borrowing homeowner. We have abolished strict foreclosure to ensure that banks can get their money back while borrowers can keep the equity they have built up in their homes. Such protective laws may increase the price of mortgages, but every state has them because they protect the legitimate expectations of borrowers and lenders alike.

I have argued that it is true that regulations may increase the costs of providing consumer goods and services. But we do not help the poor by eliminating regulations that we all need to ensure that we get what we pay for. We could lower the costs of housing by eliminating all building code regulations and allowing people to live in shacks. That would decrease the costs of housing but would deprive everyone of the security of living in safe housing. No, we ensure that market transactions provide consumers with what they have a right to expect, and we protect the poor in ways other than removing regulations that protect all of us. If some people are too poor to be able to afford minimally decent accommodations, then we have to provide them housing some other way. We do not help the poor by making the world unsafe for everyone.

The states have, for the most part, outlawed strict foreclosure for the same reason. Such regulations provide both parties to the transaction with what they have a right to expect. The new regulation of subprime mortgages similarly protects people from obligations they would not agree to if they had complete understanding of the terms of those agreements. In such a case, we are not depriving them of choices but protecting them from choices they are very likely to regret in the future. Such regulations do not deprive us of freedom; they give us the freedom to trust bankers when we approach them for a suitable loan.

"Paternalism" or Freedom?

A common concern about "regulatory laws" is that they are "paternalistic." Rather than allowing us to do what we like and choose the terms of our contracts as we please, regulatory laws prohibit us from entering certain types of agreements. That suggests that lawmakers think they know better than we do what is in our best interest. They are acting in a paternalistic fashion by not treating us as adults capable of making our own decisions. This goes against the most basic assumptions Americans have about what it means to be free. Who are you to tell me how to live my life? As long as I am not harming others, why shouldn't I be at liberty to do what I want and to make the agreements I want to make on the terms I choose?

There are two standard defenses of paternalistic laws. The first is that such laws are justified if we are protecting others from the externalities of our agreements. As we have seen, subprime mortgages had devastating effects on the economy and led to a recession that cost jobs, reduced the wealth of many, and mired us in the doldrums. It is not paternalistic to stop you from doing something that harms others. Such laws arguably do not protect you; they protect the rest of us from your shenanigans.

A second defense of such laws is that they are not paternalistic at all. They protect you from obligations you yourself would not take on if you had a perfect understanding of the relevant information. They don't deprive you of what you think you want; they give you want you really want. You may think right now that the obligations of that mortgage are affordable, but those with experience in these matters are pretty sure that when the higher payments kick in, you will regret having entered the agreement. We are not overriding your choices; we are deferring to the choices that would be made by your future self, who has a lot more experience than you do right now. Of course, we cannot be sure about this, but we have enough experience to believe that we are doing this not for your own good, but because it is what you yourself would want if you had perfect information.

There is a cottage industry of academics writing scholarly articles explaining all the ways that people are biased and irrational. Daniel Kahneman's best-selling book *Thinking, Fast and Slow* has a veritable litany of ways our understanding of the world is distorted.[27] Cass Sunstein's book *Nudge* similarly explains the utility of laws designed to push us in directions we ourselves would favor if we were not the victims of our own biases and faulty heuristics.[28]

Libertarians have long argued that markets are efficient and self-correcting and that government regulations only stop the market from doing its work to allocate resources efficiently. But psychologists like Kahneman and "behavioral economists" like Sunstein have now come to the foreground to argue that people predictably make a great many errors in judging what is in their best interests. People focus on the short term and fail to see the long-term consequences of their actions; they seize on highly visible events and misjudge the chances of those events occurring; they protect themselves from fear by assuming that harmful events are unlikely to touch them personally, etc.[29] Regulations are therefore in place to protect borrowers from entering arrangements that result in 1,000 percent interest or that are so inflexible that they lose their homes even if they can pay back their loans, with interest, two days late.

One reason for mortgage regulations is to protect us from mistakes we are likely to make and likely to regret. We have a lot of evidence of mistakes that many people make and of the regret they experience when they realize they signed a contract with onerous terms. Laws may well be passed for this reason. Social Security and Medicare, for example, may be understood as forced insurance programs. We know that we should save for retirement and end-of-life medical care, and that if we don't do this we will regret it, so we legislate programs that force us to save. This achieves our purposes and satisfies our preferences for saving while acknowledging that we would not save as much as we would like to save if we made the decision month by month rather than adopt a framework that makes saving automatic.

Mortgage regulations similarly protect us from entering agreements we think we can comply with but which have draconian penalties for noncompliance. We want protection from such contracts because we know we underestimate the chances that we will default on our mortgage payments. Such regulations do not interfere with our preferences; they satisfy them by ensuring that our long-term goals are met.

There is another, more basic reason for regulations like these. We want regulatory laws because they protect our freedom. For one thing, we must remember we have regulatory laws because we elected officials who passed them. It is peculiar and shortsighted to focus on the fact that regulatory laws may limit freedom of contract as if the only sphere in which we exercise freedom is the marketplace. We live in a democracy, and we choose our leaders. If we want to repeal the laws they have passed (because the laws take away our freedom), then we are free to do that. We have not done so because we chose the leaders who chose to enact those laws. *One way we exercise freedom is in the political sphere.* We choose laws that set the minimum standards for market relationships. We want to affect the environment within which we make choices; we want to use democratic means to shape the contexts within which we exercise our liberties.

Consumer protection laws do not paternalistically take away our freedom. They give us the benefit of things we want. It would violate our freedom to prevent us from choosing to enact laws that set minimum standards for market relationships. We want those protective laws, and it would be paternalistic for scholars to argue that we should not have them. We are entitled to exercise our freedom *as citizens* to enact laws that protect our freedoms *as consumers.*

While it is true that consumer protection laws may protect us from mistakes we are likely to regret, we choose to live with these regulatory statutes not because we are stupid or irrational and want protection from doing dumb things. We choose to enact consumer protection laws because we want protection from being cheated or treated unfairly. We demand laws because, in a free and democratic society, economic and social relationships must comport with certain minimum standards. Those minimum standards ensure that we treat each other with common decency. They ensure that deals are interpreted in light of the parties' legitimate expectations. They ensure that we do not take undue advantage of each other. They ensure that others cannot take our property on false pretenses. They protect us from being stripped of our wealth by unscrupulous malefactors or by businesses that give in to the temptation to make money any way they can.

In *The Once and Future King*, T. H. White explained King Arthur's conception of the mission of the knights of the Round Table. "What I meant by civilization when I invented it, was simply that people ought not take advantage of weakness."[30] Mortgage laws exist not because we are stupid and need to be tied to the mast like Odysseus. They exist because we know that the profit motive and economic competition may induce businesses to make money by asking customers to agree to terms that are unfair and harmful. They exist because we want laws that ensure that we get what we want and that we are not subject to preventable harm.

Free markets are undermined if we cannot trust those with whom we deal. That is why we regulate unfair and deceptive business practices. We want freedom from fear of being cheated. Free markets and private property are both undermined if businesses succumb to competitive pressures to sell loans that are likely to fail and cause harm to neighbors and the general economy.

Laws prevent us from making demands of each other that should not be made in a democratic society that treats each person with equal concern and respect. It is not true that liberty demands that all preferences be satisfied and that all actions are allowed. There are some demands that we cannot make of each other in a free and democratic society. Law exists to set those minimum standards. Regulation of the mortgage market is not an interference with personal liberty, nor is it an inefficient obstruction to social welfare. Mortgage law sets the minimum standards for fair dealing in a society that is premised on respect for the dignity of each and every person.

4

Why Private Property Needs a Legal Infrastructure

Before the laws, there was no property:
take away the laws, all property ceases.

—JEREMY BENTHAM

Conservatives oppose regulatory laws that interfere with established property rights.[1] Such laws seem not only to take what we rightfully own but to infringe on our liberty by preventing us from exercising our freedom to control what is ours. This all suggests that proponents of private property must be opponents of government regulation. Nothing could be further from the truth. Property rights do not exist without a legal framework. No regulation, no property. Property can exist only if we have relatively clear rules about who owns what. That means we need rules to allocate and define property rights. This requires a lot more law than we may imagine. Property rights also cannot be protected unless we ensure that these rights are used in ways that do not harm the personal and property rights of others; that means we must limit property rights in order to protect property rights.

They may not realize it, but Americans who profess to be champions of private property are also strong advocates of regulation.

What Kinds of Property Rights Should Be Recognized in a Democracy?

We have seen that in a free and democratic society, many types of property rights are prohibited. We outlaw feudal arrangements and slavery. We outlaw arrangements that give husbands control of their wives' property. We prohibit indentured servitude and we have (mostly) abolished debtors' prison. We do not allow property to be restricted to the use or occupancy of persons of a particular race. We do not allow "entailed" property that passes from generation to generation and cannot be freed from the control of future generations. We do not allow monopolies to choke off economic competition. We do not recognize intellectual property in ideas. We do not in general enforce "restraints on alienation" that prevent us from selling our land if we want to do so. We do not allow businesses to sell unsafe or defective products. The list goes on and on.

These regulations on the kinds of property rights that can be created serve a number of functions. They ensure that our social arrangements are compatible with the norms of a free and democratic society that treats each person with equal concern and respect. They ensure that property is not harmful to us or to our neighbors and that it comports with minimum standards consistent with our justified expectations. They ensure that most property rights are transferable. The "fee tail" form of property ownership is outlawed because it makes the property inalienable; anyone who buys the land will lose it to the seller's heir the moment the seller dies. No one will buy property under those conditions. The fee tail not only ties up the land but inhibits the freedom of the current and future generations to live where they like. Restrictions on the kinds of property rights we can create are essential to enable us to have the kinds of freedoms we cherish in a free and democratic society.

How Many Owners Should We Have?

The Hawaiian island of Lanai encompasses 141 square miles and is inhabited by only 3,135 people.[2] Ninety-eight percent of the land is owned by one man, Larry Ellison, the cofounder of Oracle Corporation. Originally owned by native Hawaiians, the land by the 1870s had mostly passed to a rancher named Walter Gibson.[3] In 1922, James Dole, president of what became the Dole Food Company, bought the island and turned it into a huge pineapple plantation.[4] In the 1980s Dole moved its operations overseas and converted the land use from agriculture to tourism. In 1985, the island's ownership passed to Dole's parent company, controlled by billionaire David Murdock.[5] Murdock sold the island to Ellison in 2012, retaining the right to construct a field of forty-five-story wind turbines over a quarter of the island. Because the tourist economy is limited by the difficulties of getting to the island, as well as harmed by the recent economic downturn following the subprime crisis, this development could form the backbone of a more robust local economy, or it could ruin the island's wild beauty—or both. The plan has sharply divided residents, who are anxious to know how the new development will affect their island.

Why tell this story? First, the most striking thing to an American is the incongruous fact that virtually all the land is owned by one person. The American conception of democracy makes us wince at this. It is reminiscent of the feudal system under William the Conqueror, who reserved the right to take back the land from his lords if they did not do as he wished.[6] When the Illinois Supreme Court considered the fact that Pullman's Palace-Car Company was the sole owner of an entire town, it interpreted state law to force the company to sell much of the land. The court explained that limiting ownership to one company is "incompatible with the theory and spirit of our institutions."[7] Recall that in colonial times, King Charles II gave New Jersey to two lords who sought to install a feudal regime only to face stalwart resistance from the settlers, who insisted on freedom from control by a feudal lord.[8] Their resistance led to the modern American system of wide dispersal of property ownership rather than allowing property to be concentrated in the hands of a small aristocracy. The settlers also helped establish our tradition of "freehold" property that confers wide powers on owners to control their own land and their own lives rather than being subject to the whim of a lord.[9]

Is there or is there not something untoward or wrong about having one owner for the entire island of Lanai? Because he is the owner, he can, with certain exceptions, choose whether to let others onto the land. He can also condition entry by inducing others to agree to his terms when they enter his land. That means that any occupants of his property are subject to his will. Whether they can even live on the island depends on what he thinks of them. Unless he decides to sell, no one else can become an owner with control of their own property. What rights do tenants and nonowners need to have so that they have some opportunity to become owners, or so that they have sufficient freedom to make their own choices about how to live? If each person is entitled to equal protection of the law, and if that means that we need to promote equal opportunity, what property law architecture is necessary to achieve that set of values? How many owners is enough? What is the appropriate balance of rights held in fee simple versus leasehold versus condominium status? Would it promote or violate property rights to take the land from Ellison and redistribute it to thousands of islanders?

Americans do not all agree about the number of owners or the mix of property forms that comports with our commitment to granting each person life, liberty, and the pursuit of happiness. Nor do we all agree about the contours of the property system that shape our choices. We have abolished feudalism, but we still have islands owned by one person, and the fact that Americans deeply value the ideal of dispersed property ownership does not mean that inequality is not an issue for us today. On the contrary, the Occupy movement placed on the national agenda the increasing inequality of wealth and income over the past thirty years.[10] The value choices here are front and center. While some argue that we should desist from "class warfare" and that it is wrong for people to be "envious" of those who are successful, others argue that inequality not only harms the economy but contradicts the American ideal of equal opportunity.[11]

When slavery was abolished, decisions needed to be made about who would own the plantations on which the slaves worked. A decision could have been made to transfer ownership to the freed persons either in individual lots or in a corporate or collective form. The slave owners who rebelled against the United States could have forfeited their property rights in the land. None of these things happened. The rebels who pledged loyalty to the United States got to keep their land, and over time less and less was done to help the ex-slaves.[12] They received neither back wages nor land of their own. What should have been done?

We are interested in the distribution of property because we care about not only satisfying our preferences at the lowest possible cost but how many people's preferences get satisfied. More than that, we care about whether we are living in a democratic or a feudal society, whether we will have freedom or servitude, whether we will have equal status before the law or titles of nobility.

Consider the continuing dilemmas in South Africa, where the antiapartheid constitution both granted a fair amount of protection to existing property owners and authorized both land reform and common law development needed to move from an apartheid society to a free and democratic one. Continuing choices need to be made that reflect not only pragmatic economic and political needs and realities but fundamental value choices. The one thing that cannot be assumed is that all "established property rights" must be protected; that would be a recipe for servitude.

Jeremy Waldron has explained that property makes liberty possible. Everything that is done, he says, must be done somewhere, and one cannot do anything unless one has a place to do it.[13] Virginia Woolf famously argued that women could not write novels until they had a room of their own.[14] If the system of property law does not make it realistically possible for each person to become an owner of the property needed for a full human life, or otherwise to have access to a place where she can be free, then we have deprived individuals of the freedom that was the reason for creating property rights in the first place. In a society that has chosen to reject apartheid as a way of life, property rights must be not only redistributed from one race to another but tailored to enable equal liberties to emerge.[15]

The question of how much inequality is appropriate cannot be answered by quantitative or economic analysis alone; rather, it implicates the meaning of the values of liberty and equality. It engages choices about the contours of a free and democratic society. Conservatives suggest that property redistribution is anathema because property is the basis of liberty; on that view, taking property inevitably takes liberty. But liberals argue that if property is necessary for the exercise of liberty, then denying property ownership denies the ability to exercise liberty; on that view, redistribution may be required to promote freedom. Determining whether our system generates sufficient opportunities to acquire property (or the abilities that property enables) implicates normative questions that can be answered only by reference to interpretation of the meaning of the fundamental values of freedom, equality, and democracy.

Who Can Own Property?

We need rules to determine who can own property and how it is allocated. The Fourteenth Amendment ensures "equal protection of the laws," and the Civil Rights Act of 1866 ensures that every citizen shall have the same right to purchase and own property as is enjoyed by white citizens.[16] The Public Accommodations Law of 1964 ensures "equal access" to certain public accommodations without regard to race.[17] And the U.S. Supreme Court case of *Shelley v. Kraemer* interpreted the equal protection clause to allow property owners to create racially restrictive covenants but denied them the power to enforce them in court.[18] The 1968 Fair Housing Act prohibited the creation of racial covenants as well as racially discriminatory refusals to sell, rent, or mortgage property because of race, religion, or national origin.[19] All these laws and decisions have embodied an antiapartheid principle at the heart of modern American property law; no one can be denied the opportunity to acquire or enjoy property because of skin color.[20] We tend to take these laws for granted in the twenty-first century, but the abolition of racial restrictions on access to property occurred in my lifetime. The Married Women's Property Acts of the nineteenth century ensured that married women could own and control their own property, and a few "community property" states gave married women equal rights to the property acquired by either husband or wife during marriage. It was not until the 1960s that most states passed statutes ensuring married women a share of the marital property accumulated during marriage, and then only upon divorce.[21]

The question of who is entitled to own property is not limited to issues of discrimination. Consider tenants who are evicted when their landlords lose their properties to foreclosure after defaulting on subprime mortgages. Should rent-paying tenants have any rights to stay in their homes? The law has traditionally said no because tenants are not owners and the new owners have the right to end periodic tenancies upon giving requisite notice.[22] But recall that homeowners were also originally not owners when they borrowed money in exchange for a mortgage on their property. Some states—like the Commonwealth of Massachusetts—retain this old-fashioned system. When you grant a mortgage to a bank in Massachusetts, the bank has title to your property until you pay off the note. Similarly, the western states that use deeds of trust rather than mortgages grant title to the property to the trustee until the debt is paid. In England, although the borrower gave the property title to the lender in exchange for the loan, if the borrower then defaulted on the loan in violation of the agreement, the equity courts intervened to protect the rights of "non-owners" from strict foreclosure; these individuals were allowed to stay on land they did not "own," even though they had defaulted on their obligations, as long as they paid off the debt in a reasonable time. Statutes in every state likewise give homeowners the right to stay in their homes and avoid foreclosure if they can make up in a timely fashion the payments they have missed. These protective rights exist even though homeowners with mortgages in states like Massachusetts and California do not have title to their homes, and even though they have missed payments they solemnly promised to make.

Why, then, don't tenants who are paying the rent have the same rights to stay in their homes after foreclosure, especially when the new owner is a bank that has no interest in moving into the home itself? In the mortgage context, we deem the bank's interest to be only in the repayment of the debt with contractually agreed-upon interest, while the homeowner's interest is a personal attachment to a home, deserving of solicitude regardless of what the contract says. As long as the bank is made whole monetarily, mortgage law gives the homeowner the right to stay in her home. Why are residential tenants denied this right? Several jurisdictions have in fact granted tenants the right to remain in their homes unless the landlord can show a legitimate reason to evict them, such as the landlord's interest in moving into the property herself.[23] Most states, however, conceptualize tenants as nonowners who have no right to continue living in their homes once the lease runs out, no matter how long they have been living there.

Massachusetts passed a statute that allows rent-paying tenants to continue to live in their homes even after foreclosure if the property is bought at foreclosure by the mortgagee-bank, as often happens. Under that law, only when the property is transferred to a third party owner is the tenant vulnerable to eviction.[24] Does this law take property rights away from the banks or does it protect the property rights of tenants? Should tenants have a right to continue living in their homes unless just cause can be shown to evict them? Should tenants be treated as the "owners" of their leaseholds, with landlords relegated to a subordinate status as future interest holders who can kick out tenants only if the landlords want to occupy the property as their home? Should rent-paying tenants be empowered to stay in their homes after foreclosure unless the new owner can demonstrate a superior interest?

Answering these questions requires us to choose the kind of social life we want to have. It requires determining whether there is a relevant distinction between defaulting homeowners and rent-paying tenants. It requires a normative analysis of the relevant interests, values, rights at stake, and the justifiability of the expectations of the parties. It requires us to determine the value we place on staying in one's home.

We need rules today to answer questions about ownership when competing claims clash. What happens if I build a fence around my property where both my neighbor and I think the border is, but we discover thirty years later that we were off by two feet? We could rely on the line as established in the written deed and confirmed by the land survey, but most states will move the line to where the fence is, based on the long-standing possession of the property enclosed by the fence. In such cases we must choose between the line defined by formal documents and the long-standing informal acquiescence or agreement among neighbors regarding the location of the border. Because so many mistakes are made about borders, the law of adverse possession generally settles boundaries where they have long been, at least when both sides have acted in good faith, and it does so to protect the justified expectations of owners.

Similar issues of allocation of property rights arise when a tenant fails to pay the rent. Ordinarily, we would think that means the landlord has the right to evict the tenant and recover possession. However, most states refuse to allow the eviction if the reason the tenant withheld rent was the landlord's failure to comply with the housing code, such as by not fixing a broken furnace needed to provide heat. Protection against eviction in such cases is premised on the notion that the landlord breached the lease first by failing to comply with the housing code. Because tenants bargain for a habitable apartment, they have the right to landlord services necessary to keep the property up to contemporary standards as defined by law.

The subprime crisis has presented the courts with myriad issues in the foreclosure context. Can a bank foreclose if it cannot produce clear written evidence that it is entitled to enforce the underlying loan? Because securitization of subprime mortgages reached a fever pitch, banks were often careless about keeping clear records of mortgage assignments. Given the millions of defaults and foreclosure procedures, some courts started enforcing a rule that is hundreds of years old. A peaceable possessor of property cannot be ejected just because there is evidence she is not the owner or is not entitled to possession. Even if you can prove she is trespassing, you cannot eject her from the property. The only private party entitled to remove a peaceable possessor from land is one who can prove she has a better title. When banks failed to present clear written evidence of how they obtained rights in the mortgage, some courts refused to allow those banks to foreclose.

The law in this area is complicated, and the complications have multiplied because of the failure of the banks to keep careful records. The courts are between a rock and a hard place. They want to enforce mortgages and protect the rights of the lenders to recover what is owed on loans they've made. But they also want to protect homeowners from wrongful foreclosure. However we resolve this issue, the point is that we cannot do it without adopting and enforcing legal rules to determine who has the right to possess the property. We need mortgage and foreclosure law; that means regulation. No regulation, no property.

How Long Do Property Rights Last?

In college, I took an introductory economics course with Professor Randall Bartlett. In one of the early classes, he asked us if we were in favor of economic competition. Having been taught that competition was a good thing, we all said yes. He looked at us and said, "Really? Would you like it if you never knew, when you came to class, whether or not there might be someone else already sitting in your seat, ready, willing, and able to do a better job than you?" Well, no, that would be nerve-wracking, we all thought. That would be like going home and finding someone else in your bed, as Dr. Zhivago did in the movie when he came home to find dozens of people living in his mansion. We all would like to know that we have a home to go home to; we would all like to know we have a seat in the class—at least until the final exams come around. Prof. Bartlett did not put it in these words but, as a property scholar, I know now that what we valued was property. We wanted a stable basis of expectation, even if that stability was temporary. We wanted a haven from the storm, time to learn, time to take advantage of the opportunity that college was.

Of course, it is not a foregone conclusion that a property law system should give us such peace of mind. I played violin in orchestras when I was a teenager and had to compete to be admitted into some of them. Auditions determined not only if you got into the orchestra but what your seat was. And more than that, at any time, one of the violinists sitting behind you in the orchestra could challenge you to an audition in an attempt to take your seat from you. You never knew, from day to day, whether someone would challenge you, play better than you, and take your seat, demoting you to a less prestigious perch. You might even be challenged by someone in the junior orchestra—a challenge with the real potential for a dramatic fall from grace. One could imagine an even more dramatic competitive system that would allow anyone—even an outsider—to compete at any moment for your seat in the orchestra. Nor is this a far-fetched notion. Few Americans have job tenure; the American system of employment at will means that most people can be fired at any time for any (nondiscriminatory) reason. And recent changes in the economy have turned many more of us into independent contractors who have even less job security than the typical employee.

Our property law system, on the other hand, does not usually work this way. If you want to buy my house, you can approach me with an offer, but I am entitled to refuse without giving you a reason. I don't have to justify myself to you. In particular, I don't have to prove I can use the property better and more efficiently than you or that I value it more than you do. And you cannot force me to sell my property to you no matter how badly you want it or how valuable the use you have in mind for it. This is a value choice made by our legal system among potential forms of social life. Do we want to organize things so you have a seat in the class with the right to graduate if you follow the rules and do the work successfully, or would we rather treat you like a day laborer or an independent contractor who has to prove yourself from moment to moment, constantly at risk of losing your spot at the college? Do we want to give owners the freedom to choose when to sell, or can we force people to sell whenever we think someone else is more deserving of the property?

Conditional ownership is not entirely foreign to American law. Recall that some federal lands sold by the United States through the nineteenth century homestead laws were conditioned on the buyer building a home on the land and working it.[25] Congress decided that the land was better used by settlers than by speculators and so Congress conditioned ownership on that basis. The common law doctrine of "relative hardship" allows you to force me to sell my land to you if you build a structure that encroaches on my property when you thought in good faith that that property belonged to you and I failed to do anything to stop you from building.[26] The common law gives you the right to take my property by adverse possession if you occupy it for a long time without my permission.[27] Sometimes the courts will even force you to sell me the benefit of a restrictive covenant you own if it interferes with the best and highest use of my property.[28] The state of Hawaii forced landowners on the island of Oahu to sell their property to their tenants because the distribution of property was so unequal that it deprived almost everyone of the chance of becoming an owner.[29] The fair use exception to copyright law prevents you from interfering with my freedom to comment on your intellectual property.[30]

In all these cases, lawmakers faced a choice between property and competition, between stability and change, between quiet enjoyment and new development. How much stability do we want and how much competition do we want? How much power should owners have to stop others from impinging on the value of their property? What obligations do owners have to the community and their neighbors? Property law systems must take positions on how much stability and how much competition to foster.

At the time of the American Revolution, it might well have been thought to be a violation of property rights for someone to open a rival store in a small town. It took a decision of the Supreme Court in the Charles River Bridge case to cement the idea in American law that there was no property right to be free from ordinary competition.[31] It took a decision by the Supreme Court of Illinois to force the Pullman Company to sell its property in Pullman, Illinois, on the ground that company towns were contrary to the "spirit of our institutions."[32] Determining how many owners is enough and how much stability to protect are choices about the nature of social and political life—choices that depend on normative reasoning about what it means to protect the freedom of individuals, to treat each person with equal concern and respect, and to live in a free and democratic society.

What Can You Do with Your Property?

Property rights cannot be absolute because we do not live alone. Our use of our property can affect the property of others. If we want to have private property, we must limit what owners do to ensure that their neighbors can enjoy their own property. We limit how people can use their property to protect their neighbors from harms caused by air and water pollution. We enact zoning laws to establish setback requirements and to limit the height of buildings. Such laws also segregate incompatible uses such as residential and industrial property. We prevent apartment tenants from making so much noise that they keep their neighbors awake at night. We enforce covenants and rules adopted by homeowners' associations or condominium associations to enable groups of neighbors to control their environment and promote mutually agreed-upon rules for the uses of common property and to protect them from incompatible uses next door. We allow owners to create businesses that compete with others even to the extent of putting them out of business, but we prevent the creation of monopolies that stifle competition.

Although we normally allow owners to choose whom to invite onto their property and whom to exclude, we prohibit retail establishments from refusing to serve customers because of their race or religion. We prevent property owners from refusing to sell, rent, or mortgage property because of the customer's race, religion, or sex. We require businesses open to the public to make them accessible to people with disabilities. We limit the right to exclude so that the right to participate in economic life—including the right to acquire and enjoy property—is not limited to those of a particular race or caste.

We establish recording offices so that property titles will be clear, and potential buyers or lenders can determine who owns property and whether it is encumbered by prior mortgages, leases, easements, or restrictions. We require most property transactions to be in writing in order to make ownership clear. We require wills to be in writing and signed with two witnesses so we do not have to resort to biased testimony to determine the deceased's intentions regarding who should inherit her property. We refuse to enforce most "restraints on alienation" that purport to limit the power of owners to transfer title to their property to others. Conversely, we allow property rights to be transferred orally or informally in certain cases when we believe it necessary to prevent injustice.

We allow the states to take property by eminent domain when needed to create highways or government office buildings. We have criminal and civil forfeiture laws that take away property when it is used for illicit purposes. We allow landlords to evict tenants who do not pay the rent, and we allow banks to foreclose on property when owners default on their mortgage payments. But we also protect most tenants from self-help evictions, which occur when landlords change the locks and exclude tenants from the premises; instead, we require eviction by court procedures, giving tenants the opportunity to show why they should not be evicted and some time to find a new home if need be, and we subject foreclosures to processes designed to ensure they are carried out fairly and appropriately.

All these regulations are only the tip of the iceberg. Much of the law school curriculum concerns regulation of property. That includes a course on the law of corporations, partnerships, negotiable instruments, secured transactions, real estate, family law, trusts and estates, taxation, bankruptcy, land use regulation, environmental law, oil and gas and energy law, water law, and federal lands management. In all these areas, we need rules to determine what packages of property rights can be created, who owns which resources, what the owners can do with these resources, and how the owners can transfer the resources to others. It takes a lot of law to answer these questions, because we have different answers for different social contexts and because we do not live alone and the use of our property has significant effects on others. Just as our liberties must be compatible with the liberties of others, our property rights must be compatible with both the property rights and the liberties of others. To have a private property system is to have a property law system, and to have property law is to embrace regulation.

Property and the Golden Rule

We do not live alone; we have neighbors. This is an obvious fact, but it is one that we sometimes forget when we think about property. For example, we often chafe at zoning laws that limit what we can do on our own land. When my family added a dining room onto our house, we not only needed to get a building permit but had to comply with zoning regulations that limited how large our new room could be. In one sense, that meant that our property rights were limited. But why was that law in effect? The law required us to keep a certain percentage of our land permeable to rain in order to avoid the flooding that would happen if the land were completely covered up by construction or asphalt. It also ensured sufficient setbacks from the borders so that the neighbors would have fresh air and be able to walk around their homes without intruding onto adjacent property. The law that limited us was intended to ensure that we did not encroach on our neighbors' quiet enjoyment of their property or build in a way that put their homes at risk. Our freedom of action was limited to protect their security. And the converse is also true; their freedom of action was limited to protect our security.

It is surprisingly easy to forget that property rights are not merely individual entitlements but a system that requires the rights of each to be compatible with the rights of others. Limits on property uses designed to protect the property rights of neighbors are not oppressive interferences with the rights of owners; they are part of what it means to have a private property system in a free and democratic society that grants each person the same basic rights enjoyed by others. A democracy holds that each person is "created equal," and that means we cannot define property rights for some in a way that allows them to destroy the property rights of others. While zoning laws limit what you can do with your property, they also protect your property rights by limiting what your neighbors can do.

Some years ago, Oregon passed a referendum that selectively deregulated property in a manner that might restrict some houses but not others on the same street. Those who voted for Measure 37 thought it would protect their property rights by not allowing any new land use restrictions to be imposed without compensation. Those who voted for the measure were imagining the benefits of being free from zoning restrictions; they thought its passage would let them develop their property or sell it to a builder for a profit. What they did not realize was that the law gave their neighbors similar rights and that it made some owners subject to regulations that other owners on the same street were not obligated to follow. When only some neighbors were freed from regulations, that meant that a house in a single-family-home neighborhood might suddenly find a tall apartment building being constructed next door, or possibly a gas station.

When owners experienced the loss of the benefits of zoning law, they realized that deregulation of neighboring property might decrease their own property values, as well as interfere with the use and enjoyment of their own homes. They had not imagined, when they voted for the law, that deregulation might harm their property rights. They had thought that they would get the benefits of deregulation (and be free to do what they liked with their own land) while retaining the benefits of regulation (they assumed that neighbors would not do anything that harmed their property enjoyment). When it was discovered that deregulation could interfere with the use and enjoyment of property, voters passed a new law substantially repealing the old one. Zoning law may be a regulatory law, and it may limit what we can do with our land, but it does so to protect our property rights, not to deprive us of them.

What Obligations Do Owners Have?

To the chagrin of the mayor, there was for a number of years a gaping hole in downtown Boston. Filene's Department Store closed and the building was purchased and then razed by the new owner. The subprime crisis soon struck and the owner either could not or would not redevelop the property. This left an ugly, empty lot in the midst of the downtown area—an eyesore that remained for several years.[33] The hole in the ground affected the surrounding area by depriving the neighbors and the community as a whole of the benefits of a business and housing that could have been profitably constructed on the property. The mayor and other city officials did what they could to convince the owner to develop the property, to no avail. The most valuable use of the property to the owner apparently was to leave it vacant and wait for the market value of the property to appreciate or the economy to recover from the Great Recession. Development may also have been contingent on banks recovering from the subprime debacle so that they would be willing to loan the money necessary for the development.

Perhaps the city could have taken the property by eminent domain and transferred it to an owner who would develop it rather than waiting for market conditions to improve. Of course, this would raise all the red flags stirred up by the much-criticized *Kelo* decision, in which the Supreme Court approved the taking of property from one owner for transfer to another as part of a neighborhood redevelopment plan. Because of widespread objection to this form of appropriation, many states changed their laws to limit such use of the eminent domain power. Taking the Filene's property would be unconstitutional in many states despite the externalities of the empty lot, while in other states the taking would be lawful only if an empty lot constituted a form of "blight." Does the owner have the right to leave the lot empty when it could be profitably developed? Does the city have the power to take the property by eminent domain to transfer it to an owner who will develop it?

This problem implicated a normative question about whether the owner was legitimately exercising his property rights or whether he was unjustifiably imposing harms on the community by his inaction. Was this an instance of a legitimate exercise of an owner's rights or was this an instance of an owner imposing negative externalities on everyone else in the city, jeopardizing their property rights and their livelihood? The dilemma was about whether the owner had the right to decide unilaterally to create a crater in the heart of the downtown area and stubbornly keep it there for years or, conversely, whether the city had the power to interfere with the owner's freedom to choose what if anything to do with his property. Was this a case of an individual freely and rationally exercising his legitimate property rights, or was it a case of an individual acting to batter and damage the property rights of others?

Suppose the city had taken the property by eminent domain, compensating its owner for its lost fair market value, and transferred it to another developer who was willing and able to redevelop the property right away. Would that be a violation of the owner's property rights? Libertarians would probably argue that owners should not have to sacrifice their property for the good of the community when the community wants to transfer the property from A to B. If the city wants the property badly enough, it should offer the owner enough to induce him to sell; if he refuses, then not only is he within his rights but we have an indication that he values the property more than others do.

The problem is, however, more complicated than this. Even libertarian philosopher Robert Nozick worried about the case of the sole owner, arguing that someone who comes to own the only water hole in the desert should have obligations to share the water with everyone else.[34] Ownership, with the attendant right to exclude others, confers power on the owner— power to deny other people things they need to live.[35] Granting the owner veto power over the decision whether to keep an empty lot in the middle of Boston's Downtown Crossing arguably violates democratic norms by giving despotic power over the community to a single individual. This situation approaches lordship. Our property norms coexist with democracy as a form of political governance; problems can arise if property rights allow the few to impose their will on the many.

Liberals would similarly have debates about the appropriate resolution of this problem. Liberals worry that majorities are likely to deprive powerless working class or poor homeowners of their homes to transfer their properties to large corporations. Liberals worry that majorities may decide to gentrify a community and displace and disperse a minority enclave. If only blighted property can be taken and redistributed, then the poor are vulnerable to having their property taken while the rich are not. How is this compatible with equal protection of the law?

On the other hand, one could classify the vacant lot as "blighted" because it impacts the local economy and is a visual and environmental blot on the center of commerce. Owners have no right to use their property to harm the property rights of others. They have no right to impose their will on the community. We live, after all, in a free and democratic society, and we do not abide lords who impose their will on the rest of us. As with the libertarian debate, liberals need to come to terms with the conflicting interests and values at stake here, including the property interests of the owner and of the neighbors who have an interest in a vibrant downtown area where they can congregate, do business, and find pleasure.

So is the owner here exercising his legitimate property rights or is he imposing harm on the community? Does he have the right to put his own interests above those of the community or does he have an obligation either to develop his property or to submit to a taking by eminent domain for transfer to someone who will develop it? These questions require normative choices among conflicting values; they also require us to interpret the meaning of those values. Would it deprive the owner of equal protection of the law to take his property because we think others could use it better, or does the owner's refusal to develop the property constitute an inegalitarian exercise of power that deprives other owners of the value of their property? Would a taking by eminent domain violate equality norms or promote them? Would it deprive the owner of the liberty to use his property as he wishes, or would it protect the quiet enjoyment of neighboring property owners by abating a nuisance? These questions implicate not only common law doctrines but constitutional norms. They represent choices about fundamental structural norms and a decision about our way of life. They represent choices about the relation between rights and power.

In a free and democratic society, owners have rights but they also have obligations. Restaurants and shops cannot exclude patrons on the basis of their race or religion. Nor can public accommodations refuse to extend reasonable efforts to make their services available to persons with disabilities. Owners are not free to ignore long-standing occupation of their property if they want to protect themselves from loss of their property by adverse possession. Owners cannot vote to pass zoning laws that unduly inhibit the ability of religious institutions to operate in their communities. Landlords cannot fail to provide tenants with heat or hot water. Owners are not free to interfere with the quiet enjoyment of neighboring owners, nor are they free to saddle buyers with covenants that unreasonably impede the alienability of the land. Owners are not free to sell property without reducing the transaction to writing and recording the documents in the registry of deeds. Nor are they free to build without complying with local building and construction codes. The number of obligations the law imposes on owners is far too great to mention. And determining what obligations owners have requires attention to our deepest norms and values.

Property law is designed to spread freedom, opportunity, security, and wealth, but it is also designed to prevent owners from inflicting harm on others and from acting in a manner that is incompatible with norms of propriety. Condominium associations, for example, are empowered to pass reasonable rules governing the use of units as well as common areas, and condominium owners are subject to those rules. But the law places limits on the kinds of rules that can be passed. Those that interfere too much with individual freedoms will be deemed outside the lawful authority of the association. For example, rules that prevent owners from displaying religious symbols on their doors may be prohibited because they violate fair housing laws that protect religious minorities from being excluded from housing.[36] The issues that can come up in this and similar contexts are almost limitless. Can condominium associations prohibit smoking entirely both in common areas and inside units? Can they prevent owners from posting signs indicating support for political candidates? Can universities prohibit students from posting political signs on their dorm windows? The Confederate flag? The Swastika? Can shopping centers exclude patrons wearing "Peace on Earth" T-shirts? Obama T-shirts? Defining the scope of property rights means defining the rights and obligations of persons in a free and democratic society.

How Markets Are Framed by the Common Law

The interconnection between property and regulation may be better appreciated if we recall why markets themselves cannot exist without a legal framework. Although we tend to imagine the free market as an arena free from regulation, an analysis of the common law rules of torts, contracts, and property shows that markets would rest on a detailed regulatory structure even if we had no regulatory statutes at all. That common law framework guarantees a great deal of freedom of action but it also limits our freedom to act as we please to protect the security of others who are affected by our actions. To mediate the tension between freedom and security, the common law allows each of us to live our own lives on our own terms but it also requires each person to be attentive to the rights of others affected by our actions. Liberals and conservatives do disagree about what the baseline rules of the market should be, but no one who is a proponent of free markets can truthfully deny that such minimum standards must exist.

In our system, we are free to live our lives as we please; each of us has the freedom to pursue happiness. Yet our free actions become problematic when they affect others. A free and democratic society does not entitle us to ignore the interests of others. Now, it is true that we have different moral codes that apply to different spheres of social life. The morality of the market is not the same as the morality of the family. Competitors put each other out of business, while family members look out for each other. Consumers try to get goods as cheaply as possible while being generous in their gifts to charitable organizations. Businesses try to cut costs, while governments spend money on basic infrastructure.

We should recognize that the morality of the market is not the same as the morality of the family or of the community, or of social life generally. At the same time, it is also true that the market has a moral code. Through both custom and law, our market system reconciles the pursuit of self-interest with the promotion of the public good by limiting our freedom of action to protect the legitimate interests of others. Corporations may be in the business of maximizing profits but they are not, and should not be, in the business of undermining the social fabric by ignoring applicable law and legitimate moral limits on their conduct. A corporation that fails to consider the impact of its activity on society and on those with whom it forms collaborative arrangements will undermine the conditions that make profit maximizing possible. More important, it will undermine the social norms that underlie our way of life.

Individuals are free to do what they please but only as long as they stay within the bounds of the law. The law governing the market system depends on background rules of contract, tort, and property law, all of which are taught in the first year of law school. What are the principles underlying those areas of law? Do they in fact stand for the proposition that, as long as one does not violate any statutory or administrative regulations, one is free to ignore the legitimate interests of others?

The answer is a resounding no. Although we are free to live our lives by our own lights, tort law is founded on the basic principle that we have an obligation to act reasonably. This obligation is most centrally established by the law of negligence, and it requires us to temper our self-interest by attending to the needs of others. We are required to abide by clear statutory and regulatory limitations on our freedom. But we are also under a continuing common law duty not to act negligently; we are not free to act unreasonably so as to foreseeably cause significant harm to others.

We are not free to ignore the interests of others as we go about our daily lives; indeed, we have a basic obligation to consider the ways in which our actions affect others. And not only do we have a duty to consider the effects of our actions on others, but we have an obligation to balance their interests against our own to determine whether we can justify the harm we may cause them. Can we explain to a neutral third party (like a jury) why we acted as we did? Can we explain to those who suffer the consequences of our actions why they suffered a tragedy but not an injustice?

Tort law is based on the fundamental notion that no one is an island and that we should do unto others as we would have them do unto us. Of course, the law cannot prohibit all harms; we would have no liberty at all if the law micromanaged our every action. The law of negligence does not turn all immoral actions into legal wrongs; we value autonomy and dignity too much to turn government into Big Brother. But the law does prohibit actions that create an unreasonable risk of harm when the harm is of a type or amount that we should not have to bear for the good of society, at least in the absence of compensation.

Perhaps surprisingly, contract law has a similar moral valence. We live in a free market system and we are entitled to pursue our own interests, to make money, to amass wealth, to profit from business opportunities created by our own labor and ingenuity. But we are not free to ignore the interests of others with whom we engage in cooperative ventures. For one thing, as we have seen, all contracts are regulated by the state; those regulations impose minimum standards on all contractual relationships to ensure that they comply with basic norms of fairness. Recall the major contracts we are likely to enter into as we proceed through life: getting a job, buying a house, getting married, buying insurance, buying consumer goods, borrowing money. Each of these contracts is regulated by state and federal statutes and regulations designed to ensure that the terms of the contracts comply with minimum standards. Those standards are designed to ensure that we get what we think we are paying for, but they are also designed to ensure that we get a certain minimum package of rights and benefits from each of those contractual relationships.

Nor are we free to do as we please once we comply with those regulatory limits. Our system of freedom of contract does not entitle us to engage in fraud or to cheat our contracting partners out of bargained-for benefits. All contracting partners are subject to fundamental obligations to refrain from dishonest conduct. The common law of fraud prohibits market actors from duping others into parting with their money by false pretenses or misleading assertions. While shareholders are protected from fraud to a much greater extent than are workers,[37] the principle is that it is fundamentally both wrong and illegal to take money from someone else under false pretenses. For this reason, all contracts are subject to a fundamental legal principle that requires us to carry out our obligations in good faith.

We have a common law and a moral duty to do what it appears we promised to do, and not to slither out of contractual obligations by finding clever loopholes in the fine print in the language of the agreement. The duty of good faith requires us to consider how our promises will be understood by our contracting partners. We are required to look out not only for our own interests, but for the interests of others with whom we have ongoing dealings. Contract law requires us to understand how others see the deal and to act accordingly. Like the negligence principle in tort law, contract law embodies a version of the Golden Rule. This is especially true when one considers the ways that consumer protection law establishes minimum standards for contract relationships to ensure that we get what we pay for and to protect our justified expectations.

Property law protects the rights of owners but it also contains other-regarding obligations. Contrary to the idea that owners have absolute rights within the borders of their property, the common law doctrine of nuisance prohibits landowners from using their own property in ways that unreasonably interfere with the use and enjoyment of neighboring land. We are not allowed to pollute our neighbors' land or cause undue noise or disturbance. Although we are free to act within the borders of our land, we are obligated to attend to the effects our actions will have on others and to refrain from acts that will cause unreasonable harm. Once again, we are not allowed to consider our own interests alone; we are required to think of the effects of exercising our property rights on both the personal and property rights of others.

In addition, property law shapes the contours of allowable ownership entitlements in a manner that is attentive to the systemic effects of property rights. Various technical principles of law (such as the rules regulating the estates systems, servitudes, leaseholds, and marital property) limit the packages of property rights we are entitled to create. They do so to ensure that ownership structures are compatible with the institutional framework of a free and democratic society that treats each person with equal concern and respect.

Property is not only an individual right but a social and economic system. If there were no limits on property rights, we could create packages of rights that would violate norms underlying our way of life. We have abolished feudalism, slavery, the rights of husbands to control the property of their wives, racial segregation, the establishment of a religion as the basis for government and law, and economic monopolies. Traditional common law rules of property, combined with statutory regulations, ensure that property rights are structured so as to promote widespread ownership of property, as well as norms of autonomy, privacy, associational freedom, and equality. The law of property is not indifferent to the effects of exercising property rights or on the structure of those rights themselves. Indeed, core principles of property law seek to ensure that our market system spreads opportunity, prevents harm, and demonstrates respect for the interests of all participants in the system.

All the basic areas of law governing the market system, including tort, contract, and property law, rest on the idea that we are obligated to attend to the effects our actions have on others; this obligation of attentiveness applies not only to the interests of strangers, but to those with whom we form continuing market relationships, and those with whom we fashion other relationships of trust. These obligations are not merely moral claims; we enforce them through common law. Both markets and property rights work because we set rules of the game that establish and protect justified expectations and ensure that the liberty of each is compatible with the liberty of all.

How Banks Undermined Property Titles

The subprime debacle taught us anew that we need consumer protection laws to protect us from deceptive mortgage practices and onerous obligations. The subprime crisis has taught us something else as well: for the institution of private property to work, we need laws that ensure the clarity and publicity of property titles.

The law seeks to protect housing consumers by making sure that they have clear title to their property. Without knowing who owns property, we can neither use our property nor sell it. To make sure we have clear title to our property, the law requires property transactions to be put in writing, and the law encourages such transactions to be filed in government offices to provide public records of who owns each piece of land and how the land is encumbered by mortgages, long-term leases, and liens.

We have had a well-working title recording system in the United States since the 1600s. The first statute of frauds was passed in England in 1677; it required property transactions to be reduced to a formal writing. The Middlesex County Registry of Deeds in the Commonwealth of Massachusetts was established in 1636; it allowed owners to record deeds and mortgages to ensure public notice of them.[38] The recording system protects homeowners by enabling them to use and sell their property without interference from others; it promotes purchase and sale as well by ensuring buyers that they will get what they think they are purchasing and will protect them from being surprised about encumbrances they did not know about.

Amazingly, over the past fifteen years, the banks have substantially undermined that system by failing to keep clear records of mortgage assignments. Moreover, they privatized the system of mortgage registration so that public records of mortgages are no longer available.[39] The formality and publicity rules skirted by the banks were not archaic relics of a primitive society; they are the foundation of our property system and can be avoided only when doing so is necessary to avoid systemic risk or substantial injustice. The banks must learn from the past as well as from recent lawsuits complaining of misrepresentation, robo-signing, and sloppy record keeping.[40]

Recording of property transactions is generally not required to effect a transfer of title or to grant a mortgage in property. A deed or a mortgage validly created and delivered effects a transfer of property rights. The same is true of subsequent sales or assignments of the mortgage. Nonetheless, the rules governing the recording system create strong incentives to record interests in real property because doing so protects the buyer from fraudulent or duplicative transfers or encumbrances. For similar reasons, mortgages are ordinarily recorded.

Mortgage assignments, however, constitute a special case. Mortgages create a security interest in property to ensure payment of an underlying debt that is formalized in a note. Negotiable instruments law in Article 3 of the Uniform Commercial Code regulates most but not all mortgage notes. They may be transferred the way one transfers rights in a check. One can endorse the note by signing it and giving the note to the transferee; one can endorse it to the order of a particular person; or one can endorse it in blank with the name of the transferee to be filled in later. Alternatively, one can simply transfer the note without endorsing it while providing independent evidence that the recipient is being granted the right to enforce the note.[41] If the right to enforce the note is transferred, the transferee would also want to be able to use the mortgage foreclosure process to enforce that obligation. In general, whoever has rights in the note also has rights to the mortgage method of enforcing the note (i.e., foreclosure). If one were careful about all this, a mortgage assignment would be drafted and recorded while the note would be endorsed and delivered to the mortgage assignee. But the banks were not careful about any of this.

While the incentive to record deeds has always been strong, the incentive to record mortgage assignments has been less strong in many states.[42] That is because the states allow the possessor of the note (or someone who can show they are entitled to enforce the note) to foreclose on the property even if there is no written mortgage assignment. The subprime market involved numerous transfers of mortgages. If the banks had foreseen the millions of foreclosures that would occur, they might also have foreseen that courts would seek assurances that the bank seeking to foreclose had a right to do so. If they had anticipated this, the banks would have kept careful records of mortgage assignments, ensured easy and assured access to the underlying note either by keeping it themselves or giving it to a custodian who could find the note when needed, endorsing the notes correctly and completely, and recording mortgage assignments to give homeowners a way to determine who currently holds rights in the mortgage and the note to facilitate negotiation in cases of default. But none of that happened.

To reduce the costs associated with securitization of mortgages, the banks invented MERS, the Mortgage Electronic Registration Systems.[43] This corporation was designed to stand in for the bank that actually issued the mortgage loan and other banks to which it might transfer the mortgage; MERS would allow the banks to avoid recording mortgage assignments every time those mortgages were transferred from one to another. In the olden days, if you borrowed money from the Bank of America to buy a house, you signed a note that constituted a contract between you and the bank stating the amount of the loan and the repayment terms. You also gave the bank a mortgage to the property, allowing the lender to foreclose on the property in either a judicial or a nonjudicial proceeding if you defaulted on your mortgage payments. That mortgage document would name Bank of America as the mortgagee and it would be recorded. If Bank of America assigned its rights in the mortgage to another bank, a written mortgage assignment would be drafted, signed, and recorded, and the note would be endorsed (signed) and transferred to the possession of the new mortgage holder. While it is true that recording of the mortgage assignment was not required, it was advisable to do so both to protect against fraudulent transfers and to ensure public notice of encumbrances attached to the land.

Instead of doing this, the MERS system allowed the original mortgage to be placed in the name of MERS rather than the Bank of America. If you went to the public registry of deeds to see if there were any liens or encumbrances on the property, you would see that the owner had granted a mortgage to MERS as "nominee" for Bank of America (the original lender). Theoretically, MERS would keep an electronic database that would list Bank of America as the real mortgagee of the property; it would also list the name of any loan servicer hired by Bank of America to collect the mortgage payments from the homeowner.

When Bank of America transferred the note and mortgage to a second bank, say Cambridge Trust, the theory was that Cambridge Trust would notify MERS and MERS would change the name of the mortgagee for that property on its books. Nothing would need to be changed in the public registry of deeds, however; since MERS was holding the mortgage as the "nominee" for the real owner, no new recording would be needed. Yet MERS also maintained, inconsistently, that it was both the mortgagee and merely the "nominee" (a limited agent) for the real mortgagee.[44] This system effectively created a national electronic registry for mortgages, bypassing the need for new paper assignments recorded in the various state registries of deeds with their attendant fees. Using this method, the banks thought they could both comply with state recording acts and avoid the costs and complexity associated with them.

The MERS system failed in several ways.[45] The banks tried to have their cake and eat it too by giving MERS inconsistent statuses in the document that created the original mortgage. That document stated that MERS was both the "mortgagee" and the "nominee" for the real mortgagee, i.e., the bank that issued the loan and took the security interest (the lien) in the property to ensure repayment of the loan. This is like claiming to be both the parent and the child, the husband and the wife, the employer and the employee, the landlord and the tenant. A contractual relationship requires two parties, and one cannot make a contract with oneself. The mortgagee is the "owner" of the mortgage; it is the one that is granted the mortgage in the property. The nominee is the agent of the mortgagee empowered to act on the mortgagee's behalf. One cannot be both the principal and the agent. If MERS is the agent (nominee) for the lender, it cannot be the lender; if it is the lender (mortgagee), it cannot be the agent (nominee).

Because MERS claimed inconsistent statuses for itself, its documents were bound to confuse the courts that were later asked to interpret those documents in foreclosure proceedings. Property law regulates the packages of rights we are allowed to create so that we can understand what we are getting when we buy or rent. Mortgage law protects banks by giving them the right to foreclose on property if the homeowner/borrower defaults on mortgage payments and to use the sale proceeds from the foreclosure to get the rest of its loan back. Mortgage law protects the borrower by ensuring that any equity in the property in excess of the unpaid loan will be retained by the borrower rather than seized by the bank. For this system to work, it must be clear who has the right to foreclose on the property and who has the right to the rest of the loan payments.

Because the MERS documents suggested that MERS was both the one to whom the loan was owed and merely an agent for the real lender, the courts have had a devil of a time trying to figure out what rights each of the parties has. If MERS is the mortgagee, it should be able to transfer the mortgage without the consent of anyone else, but if it is merely an agent for the current mortgagee, then it cannot do anything unless its principal (the current mortgagee) orders it to act. The documents were intended to give MERS the freedom to foreclose on behalf of the current mortgagee, but they were worded badly. Because of their confusing wording, the arrangement left the banks vulnerable to varying court interpretations of the rights of the parties. Some courts held that MERS could not be both the mortgagee and the nominee for the mortgagee, denying MERS the power to foreclose on the property and requiring the real mortgagee to show a chain of mortgage assignments from the original lender.[46] When banks that were trying to foreclose could not show how they acquired the mortgage rights, the internally inconsistent contract arrangements wound up hurting the banks by denying them rights in the property rather than giving them the flexibility they had sought.

The banks apparently did not carefully research state property law. They operated in the context of a national or international securities market; they did not focus on the fact that property law is state law. Every state has a Uniform Commercial Code that regulates negotiable instruments, and many courts interpret those laws to apply to many housing loan notes. Every state has statutes that allow for and regulate the recording of real property titles and mortgages. Every state has statutes that regulate the foreclosure process. The states' laws are not uniform.[47] It might be possible to develop a business model that would satisfy the rules of every state, and the banks that established MERS clearly thought they had accomplished that. In retrospect, it is clear that they did not understand or research the complexities of state foreclosure law. Foreclosure litigation is now revealing that the MERS system, as implemented by the banks, often did not comply with the requirements of the laws of the several states.[48]

The MERS system made the banks complacent. They thought that if they ever had to foreclose, then either MERS could bring the foreclosure proceedings itself, or MERS could assign the mortgage to the bank that had obtained foreclosure rights from earlier holders of those rights, and then that party (or the loan servicer) could conduct the foreclosure. The banks did not think there was a reason to have a clear chain of title showing the written mortgage assignments from the first mortgagee to the current one that was seeking to foreclose. Nor were they sufficiently careful about endorsing and storing the underlying note so that it would be accessible if needed for foreclosure. The banks also securitized and transferred so many mortgages that they made mistakes in record keeping. Their records are incomplete in some cases and inaccurate in others.[49] They failed to carefully document all the mortgage transfers, and they lost or misplaced notes. They overly relied on the MERS mechanism. In the past, the courts had always been solicitous of the banks. Most homeowners never contested foreclosures because they were indeed behind in their payments and neither the borrowers nor the courts had any reason to question whether the foreclosing bank had a right to do so.

The subprime crisis changed all of this. When people stopped being able to pay the higher interest rates associated with adjustable rate mortgages and the housing bubble burst, making refinancing impossible, defaults skyrocketed and foreclosures along with them. For the first time, homeowner/borrowers started questioning whether the bank bringing the foreclosure action was entitled to recover the property to pay off the debt. It is a settled principle of real property law that a peaceable possessor is entitled to remain in possession unless someone can prove they have a better title. But when MERS began bringing foreclosure proceedings, homeowners' lawyers began to focus on the inconsistent statuses MERS claimed for itself. The mortgage documents suggested that MERS occupied both the roles of mortgagee and nominee for the mortgagee. This is a form of property right that is not recognized by the courts; it is confusing and contradictory. The courts therefore were put to the task of determining what role MERS actually had.

Most courts realized that MERS was not actually the mortgagee even though the original mortgage agreement said it was the mortgagee. Because that document also said it was a "nominee" for the first lender, the courts understood that MERS was merely an agent for the real mortgagee. But an agent's powers cannot exceed those of the principal. For MERS to foreclose, it had to show that it was an agent for the real mortgagee.[50] But how could it do that? It would have to show a clear chain of title to the mortgage from the original mortgagee to the current mortgagee, or it would have to be able to produce the note. Because its records were unclear or incomplete, it could not always prove that it was the agent of the bank seeking to foreclose on the property when that bank was not the original lender, as usually was the case.[51] Because MERS was not designed to be a document custodian, it did not have possession of the note. Moreover, like public recording systems, its information was only as good as the information it received. If banks did not notify it of mortgage assignments, then its records would be inaccurate or incomplete. That is, in fact, what occurred in many cases.

Many states have allowed MERS to bring foreclosure proceedings in its own name.[52] They view the MERS system as beneficial to the real estate market and feel that the homeowner had agreed to let MERS act as an agent for the real mortgagee, whoever that was. So they shifted the burden of proof onto the homeowner to show that MERS was not acting on behalf of the real party in interest. Other courts, however, have refused to let MERS bring foreclosure proceedings on the ground that it had no title to the property or any interest whatsoever.[53]

If you are going to eject people from their home, you have to show you have a better right to their property than they do. But MERS has no property rights of any kind; it does not own the mortgage or have a right to enforce the note, and it is not the one to whom the loan is owed. The courts found that MERS could not be both the mortgagee and the nominee for the mortgagee, and they held that it was merely a nominee. Because MERS is not the mortgagee, it arguably has no power to assign rights in the mortgage to the real owner of the mortgage to enable that entity to foreclose unless MERS is acting as the agent for some principal.[54] If MERS is serving as the agent (nominee) for the real mortgagee, it cannot serve in that capacity without a clear record of who its principal is.[55] For the same reason, some courts refused to allow loan servicers to foreclose unless they could show a chain of mortgage assignments giving them the right to foreclose as agents for the mortgagee.[56] They also were agents for a principal, and unless they could show that the principal had rights in the mortgage, they were in no better position than was MERS.[57]

That left the current mortgagee to bring the foreclosure proceeding itself. But again, in the case of judicial foreclosures, some courts started insisting on proof that the mortgagee actually possessed rights in the property at the time the foreclosure proceedings began. Because of the sloppy record keeping and the undue reliance on the MERS system, some banks could not make that showing.[58] In the case of nonjudicial foreclosures, the bank would conduct the foreclosure; usually it would buy the property itself at the foreclosure sale. At that point, title shifted from the mortgagor or the deed of trust owner to the foreclosure purchaser (usually the bank that thought it held the mortgage). That new owner would then try to evict the homeowner, who no longer had title to the property. In these cases, once again, some courts put brakes on the whole affair.[59]

If the foreclosure was conducted by an entity that was not the real mortgagee, then it had no right to foreclose on the mortgage. You can foreclose on your own mortgage but not on someone else's mortgage. I can give you a deed to the Empire State Building and you would get what I have the right to sell—which is nothing, since I do not own the Empire State Building. It is a staple of real property law that, absent a statute to the contrary (such as recording acts), you cannot convey more than you own. So if the bank that conducted the foreclosure did not own the mortgage, it could not foreclose and certainly could not transfer title to itself as foreclosure buyer. Since it obtained no title, it now had no right to eject the homeowner because it could not prove it had a better title to the property than that of the peaceably possessing homeowner.

Potential Solutions to Foreclosure Dilemmas

What to do now? Courts could strictly enforce the statute of frauds and hold that the banks simply cannot foreclose if they cannot prove that they "own the mortgage" through showing a clear chain of mortgage assignments, possession of an endorsed note, or proof that they are entitled to enforce the note. They would lose their interest in all such properties. Is that a viable solution to this problem? One problem is that this would reduce the market value of mortgages the bank cannot prove it owns to zero. That, in turn, would reduce the capital held by the bank and require it to replace that capital if needed to meet regulatory requirements to have a certain amount of money on hand. If it cannot replace that capital, there is a chance the bank could become insolvent. If this is a problem many banks face, and if many of them become insolvent, we could plunge the economy into a second major recession unless we bail out the banks a second time.

A second major issue that would arise is that the mortgagee might lose its interests in the mortgage but this would not necessarily clear title for the borrower/mortgagor. There would still appear to be an undischarged mortgage on the books in MERS's name. That means the property appears still to be encumbered by a mortgage. Just because the current mortgagee cannot prove it has title does not mean a prior assignee of the mortgage could not show a complete chain of title.

The result of all this is that the title to the property is under a significant cloud. The property seems to be subject to a mortgage in MERS's name, but since MERS cannot be the mortgagee, then the encumbrance on the property cannot be clearly identified.[60] Because the banks did not strictly comply with the statute of frauds and customary practice under the recording acts, because they often cannot produce a properly endorsed note, and because the possessor of the note may not be the person entitled to enforce the note, some mortgagee at some point could come forward and claim rights in the property under the note and mortgage through a full chain of title, but until that happens the property has an uncertain encumbrance. In conjunction with the costs of a quiet title suit or enhanced title insurance, we have impediments to the title that could render the property unmarketable.[61]

One could argue that this description of the whole problem is overblown. We should just let MERS (or whatever bank purports to hold the current mortgage) foreclose and then let the banks fight about who gets the money. The problem is that this solution privileges the bank's right to foreclose over the homeowner's right not to be evicted except by someone who can clearly and unambiguously prove a better title. However one views that normative choice, we cannot escape making a judgment about how to construct property rights in a situation like this. "Deregulating" and "letting the market take care of it" is not an option because in this instance the question is identifying the rules of the game for participating in the market. Are owners vulnerable to losing their homes to anyone who comes along who can prove they are in default on their mortgage payments? Or are owners entitled to peaceable possession of their property until someone else can show clear evidence of better title?

Given the fact that the homeowner's title is under a cloud if the bank cannot foreclose, we have a situation in which both the homeowner and the current purported mortgagee have some bargaining power over each other. The mortgagee may want to foreclose or renegotiate the mortgage payments since it needs the money from the property to fulfill its capitalization requirements and to lessen any loss of profits from its investment in the property. The homeowner needs to clear title so she can sell the property or get a new loan and fix her credit rating. Each party has an incentive to reach an agreement since both would like to clarify title.

But, of course, negotiations between them could fail for any number of reasons: they mistrust each other; they are mad at each other; they overestimate the other side's reserve price. And if the mortgage is held by a trust as part of a securitization, that trust may be subject to contractual limitations on its ability to renegotiate mortgages while the thousands of investors in the securities have no ability to contact each other, much less agree on a course of action.[62] Moreover, even if the current mortgagee and mortgagor reach agreement, that does not change the fact that under the law, the two of them cannot divest a prior mortgagee of any persisting interest in the property. Remember that if we strictly enforce the statute of frauds and require property interests (including mortgage assignments) to be in writing, then a current mortgagee that cannot show a full chain of mortgage assignments, or that cannot prove that it is entitled to enforce the note, may own nothing if state law requires such evidence. In that case, the mortgage may belong to another bank, and the homeowner cannot free herself from that mortgage simply by saying so. An agreement between the parties cannot discharge the rights of a prior mortgagee.

The courts get around all this by allowing the bank that purports to have the right to foreclose to file an affidavit swearing that it is the current lawful holder of the mortgage and the note, while public notice of foreclosure serves to place prior mortgagees on notice that they may lose their rights if they do not appear to assert them. But once again, in an effort to save costs, some banks hired people to sign hundreds of affidavits a day. They did so with no research whatsoever.[63] This "robo-signing" not only was a fraud on the court but constituted perjury. For this to work the way it is supposed to, the banks actually have to research each mortgage, find the note, and explain the evidence that leads the bank to believe that it actually has the right to foreclose on the property. But if there is no clear chain of title, and the note has been lost, what evidence would suffice? By definition, we are in this position only because the written chain of evidence is broken or incomplete. The affidavit constitutes a sworn testimony that the bank believes what it contains, but it must be backed up by objective facts and evidence. It is not clear the banks have sufficient ability to carry this out in all cases. But if they do come up with reliable evidence, and we allow them to claim the mortgage by an affidavit, notice that we have fixed the title problem by relaxing the statute of frauds.

We are forgiving the bank for failing to comply with formality requirements by reducing all the transactions to clear written form. And we are doing so because strict adherence to formality would muddy property titles rather than clarify them.

An alternative to relying on written mortgage assignments is to rely on the note as the basis for foreclosure. Whoever possesses that note (or has a contract making it the agent of the note holder) arguably has the rights in the accompanying mortgage. Traditionally, "the mortgage follows the note."[64] The note is the primary legal obligation and the mortgage is simply a device to protect the interests of the note holder. Also traditionally, when the mortgage is assigned to another bank, the note should be endorsed and transferred along with it. But what if that doesn't happen? This was a common occurrence in the subprime mortgage market. Some courts hold that the mortgage and the note cannot be owned by different parties.[65] But what happens if they are separated? Most courts say the note holder's rights are primary and the mortgage holder holds those rights for the benefit of the note holder.[66] A few courts say the holder of the mortgage owns it and along with it the rights under the note on the ground that a mortgage assignment intends to transfer rights in the note.[67] Some states hold that the foreclosing party must possess both the mortgage and the note or be in an agency relationship with the note holder.[68] Some states had clear rules about this prior to the subprime crisis, but others did not.[69]

The banks assumed that the courts would trust them and allow them to foreclose on properties when homeowners defaulted on their loans. But because they issued subprime loans that resulted in millions of foreclosures, and because the banks diverged so sharply from prior practice by creating MERS, the banks took a risk that the courts would not interpret state law to validate their arrangements. Their lack of care in documenting mortgage transfers and keeping track of notes was their undoing. They did not anticipate that courts would both hold them to traditional statutory formality requirements and burdens of proof and rule in favor of homeowners and against the banks' interests. Because of the failures to document mortgage assignments clearly and keep clear custody of notes and transfer them in proper ways, and because of the robo-signing scandal, many judges no longer trust the banks.

The old system worked because the courts trusted the banks, and now that this trust is gone, we are beset by dilemmas. The banks did not realize that an efficient and well-working market system depends on trust, both among market actors and contracting parties and between market actors and government regulators, including judges. The banks cut corners, and many judges are in no mood today to cut them slack. To make things worse, many states allow nonjudicial foreclosure; that system is much less expensive than judicial foreclosure and it especially depended on courts and legislators trusting banks to exercise their powers appropriately. But now that trust in banks has been shattered, eviction lawsuits following nonjudicial foreclosure are reintroducing the costs that nonjudicial foreclosure was supposed to avoid.

Amazingly, over the past ten years, the banks have wrecked a property recording system that worked relatively well for hundreds of years.[70] It is astonishing that they did this and tragic that we are suffering the price of their arrogance. We are left today with clouded titles, rampant litigation, and insecure property rights. All this inhibits the use and alienability of land. The banks' practices violated core norms underlying private property law.[71] The banks thought they could make money by getting around the rules or even by ignoring them. We had clear rules, but the banks ignored them. Clear rules did not lead either to clear titles or to predictable results.

That leaves us with a paradox. If we do not have a writing requirement for property transactions, then property rights will not be clear; people can always claim they acquired rights by informal arrangements or oral contracts, and it is easy to lie about such things. But if we strictly enforce the writing requirement, title will also not be clear; because of the massive refusal to comply with the writing requirement and because of the importance of mortgages to the banks' capital structure and bottom line, strict enforcement of the writing requirement will either cause a new recession or generate massive lawsuits to renegotiate property rights. We're damned if we do and damned if we don't. If we don't have formal writings, we don't have clear title, but if we strictly enforce the writing requirement, we don't have clear title either. Rigid rules, including rules governing formalities, do not necessarily lead to clear property rights even if you attempt to apply them mechanically. Rules do not promote predictability or clear property rights if people do not follow them; this turns out to be a far more serious problem than we may have thought.

Why Private Mortgage Records Undermine Property Rights

The MERS system failed not only because it led to careless record keeping and was carried out in a manner that violated the real property law of some states, but because it privatized information about mortgages. State recording acts generally promote but do not require interests in real property to be recorded to be valid. A few states, like Pennsylvania, do require real property interests not only to be in writing but to be recorded to be legally valid.[72] Most states rely on the self-interest of mortgage lenders to record mortgages to ensure that they have priority over later interests. The system not only promotes a clear record of who owns property and what encumbrances attach to it, but makes that information available to the general public. This means that anyone who wants to buy property or provide a loan secured by a mortgage in the property can determine who owns the property and what prior liens exist on it. Making the information public serves the old-fashioned goals of property law by promoting the alienability of land. While mortgage assignments were not always recorded before the subprime crisis, MERS complicated things enormously by seeking to occupy an ambiguous status in the mortgage system and by inducing privatization of mortgage information.

Because only MERS's name and that of the original lender appear in the public records, there is no longer publicly available information about who owns particular mortgages; that information is all on MERS's private computers.[73] Until recently, MERS did not even make that information available to the

homeowners who were obligated to pay the mortgages; all
MERS would tell homeowners was the name of the loan servicer
hired to collect their payments.[74] For that reason, the homeowner who wanted to avoid foreclosure by negotiating with
the beneficial owner of the mortgage could not find out who
that was either by searching public records or by consulting
MERS.[75] MERS has now partially changed that policy but it still
does not make mortgage ownership information available to
the public; it will not tell strangers who owns the mortgage in a
particular piece of real estate.[76] Nor will MERS reveal the chain
of title so potential buyers of land can determine if the current
mortgage holder could foreclose on the property if it sought to
do so.

What effects does this new secrecy of property titles have?
For one thing, homeowners seeking to renegotiate their mortgages could not do so when MERS would not tell them who
owned the mortgage. MERS would tell them only the name of
the loan servicer, and loan servicers often had incentives to
foreclose rather than renegotiate.[77] The loan servicers' contracts
often gave them more money that way, and sometimes the contracts prohibited them from renegotiating the deal.[78] But even
though MERS has changed that policy, neither the homeowner
nor others can determine what encumbrances there are on the
property. Because of past business practices by both MERS and
the banks, neither homeowners, potential buyers, the banks
themselves, nor the courts have any reason to treat MERS
records as either complete or accurate. And since they cannot
trust those records, they seek information about the actual

chain of transactions affecting the property. But MERS does not have that information because the parties did not provide it. Moreover, it treats its computers and the information on them as private property from which it has the right to exclude outsiders. The result of all this has been to destroy our public recording system. We no longer have trustworthy public records of property title in the United States.

Property scholars have long argued that property rights cannot work if they are not clear.[79] They have also recently emphasized that they cannot work if they are not publicly known. Henry Smith's work on the in rem nature of property rights emphasizes the information cost benefits of knowing who is the gatekeeper for property.[80] Privatizing information in property rights requires us to trust MERS to be accurately determining who the current mortgagee is. But we have no reason to trust MERS both because the records are not public and because the MERS system induced banks to fail to keep complete and accurate records of mortgage assignments.

While freedom of contract is traditionally assumed to be the core value of our contract law system, promoting the alienability of land is traditionally assumed to be the core value of our property law system.[81] That policy supports giving owners robust powers over their property, and it requires clear rules about who owns what; that means public notice of who owns land and how it is encumbered. In their zeal to make money, the banks have broken the foundational structures on which our property law system sat. They viewed regulations as costly interferences with their pursuit of profit, and they failed to understand how those regulations were necessary for the property market to work well in the first place.

Our property system cannot work unless we have clear, public records of title to property. That includes written records of all encumbrances on the land, such as easements, covenants, liens, mortgages, and court judgments. People cannot use or develop their property if ownership is unclear, and their property cannot be marketed if it is unclear whether the property is subject to an outstanding mortgage and who the identity of the mortgagee is. There are many desirable exceptions to this principle, but they are exceptions.[82] Those exceptions apply in fairly well-defined circumstances and are designed to protect legitimate expectations. With regard to mortgages, knowing who owns property and what mortgages validly attach to it not only makes property alienable but protects consumer interests in knowing with whom to negotiate in the event of default and in protection from eviction by anyone who does not have a superior title to the land.[83]

Re-creating Clear, Public Property Titles

The bottom line is that property titles must be sufficiently clear and public. There are various ways to achieve these goals. To some extent, the clarity issue is likely to be improved in the future by the banks exercising greater care in documenting mortgage transactions. They have experienced firsthand the problems that ensue when they cannot prove they have a right to foreclose on property. Not only does this affect their ability to enforce their rights, but it has the potential to affect the banks' capital requirements and poses a risk to the banks' solvency. At the same time, the states should consider adopting the Michigan approach to nonjudicial foreclosures by requiring proof of the "record chain of title . . . prior to the date of sale . . . evidencing the assignment of the mortgage to the party foreclosing the mortgage."[84] State laws may also need to be updated not only to make electronic records more easily available but to ensure their authenticity.

If MERS is going to continue to be used as a national registration system for mortgages, we need to change its practices to restore the publicity of land titles. Since it has not voluntarily done this, we may need a law to require MERS to make its records public.[85] The state recording systems were devised to create incentives to induce buyers and lenders to record deeds and mortgages in a public office. This lets any potential buyer determine who owns the property and what encumbrances or restrictions are attached to it. The MERS system privatizes this information. Because the banks were so careless with their records of mortgage assignments and their custody of notes, and because there is evidence that MERS records are often inaccurate, there is no reason to trust the MERS records. The only way to regain trust is to induce banks to be more careful about mortgage assignments and rights in the notes, and to make the chain of title accessible to potential buyers.

As Alan White argues, "a better system design would incorporate transparent and authoritative registration of mortgage loan ownership throughout the life of the loan, and not just at the point foreclosure is initiated."[86] Property will not be alienable if buyers cannot trust that they will actually own the property they think they are buying. If that property is possibly subject to outstanding liens of which they are unaware, they will be discouraged from buying the land. If MERS is going to be our repository of information about mortgage transactions, there is no way to achieve these goals without forcing MERS records to become both complete and accessible to the public.

The traditional recording system worked by giving banks an incentive to record their mortgages. The MERS system arguably weakened that incentive by giving banks the impression that it was not necessary to notify MERS whenever mortgages were assigned. Because the courts have not fully accepted the MERS system, we have a renewed incentive for banks to notify MERS about mortgage transfers. That means that MERS must track not only the current mortgage holder but the history of assignments from which that entity derives its rights. Traditionally, those assignments would be accomplished both by endorsement of the note and by a mortgage assignment. Banks must figure out how to comply with these requirements or seek law reforms that might simplify them.

If some states continue to allow the current mortgagee to foreclose simply by showing an assignment of the mortgage from MERS, we need to establish a requirement that banks register mortgages for them to be valid, either by recording them in public recording offices or by notifying MERS of the transfer. The subprime crisis shows that what we need are clear, public records of both the original mortgage and subsequent assignments. If MERS cannot be reformed to accomplish these goals, then a federal public agency should be created to take its place preempting state law to the contrary. Such an agency could insist on appropriate regulation of mortgage transfers while preserving the accessible, public notice of mortgage liens.

Changes are needed to the Uniform Commercial Code and state foreclosure statutes to clarify the relationship between negotiable instruments law and mortgage law. Because it may be useful for one party to hold the note and another to hold the mortgage, we need clearer answers to the question of which party is the principal and which is the agent. We also need clarification of how mortgage transfers should occur. Traditionally, whoever has the right to enforce the note has the right to foreclose to enforce the note, but state law has been less than clear about how mortgage assignments should happen. Banks could have avoided problems by formally endorsing notes, keeping them, and producing and recording mortgage assignments. They failed to ensure adequate formality to these transactions; that is what we need to restore. In some sense, it does not matter how we do so; we just need the law to help make this possible and facilitate it.

If the states agree on the underlying principles and procedures, then state law could be made uniform (by common law or a uniform act) to effectuate the shared norms. In general, the courts assume that the mortgage serves the interests of the note holder; the mortgage is security for the loan. The states differ on whether the transfer of the mortgage brings the note with it or the mortgage holder holds it for the benefit of the note holder. They also differ on what acts are sufficient to prove who is an agent for another principal. The courts are wrestling with these issues now, and they are among the issues that were not completely clear before the subprime crisis. Both clarity and uniformity would be desirable in this area.

Various approaches could achieve these goals. Back in 2002, Dale Whitman argued for a uniform electronic recording act.[87] He has recently recommended a federally created national mortgage registry to correct the deficiencies in the MERS system.[88] Adam Levitin has argued for a national registry of mortgage notes, while Alan White has argued that we should merge the note and the mortgage into a single document that could be more easily tracked.[89] Dustin Zacks has suggested that MERS should be "forc[ed] to store actual electronic documents that were previously recorded at the local recording level, such as mortgages and assignments."[90] And Tanya Marsh has argued for nationalizing the title registration system, effectively replacing both state recording offices and MERS with a public federal system of title and mortgage registration.[91] Rather than choose among these proposals, I simply want to applaud them for suggesting ways to achieve the ultimate goal: to restore our system of clear, public titles that the banks have destroyed.

Property and the Rule of Law

Just as we tend to think of markets and regulations as mortal enemies, we imagine that regulations infringe on our property rights by limiting what we can do with our things. We think of regulations as taking away both our freedom and our property. But neither markets nor private property can exist without a legal framework. And because we embrace the values of a free and democratic society, property rights must be defined by law so as to ensure that they enable us to keep what is rightfully ours and to enjoy equal opportunity to acquire property and to participate in economic life. Because we do not live alone, we need laws that establish minimum standards for market relationships and we need laws that limit what we can do with our property so that it does not destroy the property of others. Because we want to be free from fear, we regulate the packages of property rights we are entitled to create so that they do not harm others and so that property titles are both clear and public.

We need laws to shape the contours of property rights so that we have the ability to pursue happiness and the security of knowing that others cannot use their property in ways that upset our justified expectations. To have a private property system is to have a system of property law, and to have property law is to embrace regulation. The banks tried to make money by marketing subprime mortgages, but that backfired when borrowers were unable to pay back loans they could ill afford. The banks tried to save money by privatizing the mortgage registration system, but that also backfired when the banks were careless in record keeping and could not prove ownership of mortgages when they needed to do so to foreclose on them. Our property system cannot exist and cannot work properly if property rights are not created, formalized, and transferred in accordance with workable rules. The banks forgot this fact. They looked at regulations as things that stopped them from engaging in profitable transactions. They looked at regulations as limitations on their property rights. They forgot—or did not realize—that *without regulation, they would have no property rights.* Again, regulations can be stupid and harmful; what we need are the right regulations. But property without regulation is an impossibility.

5

Why Conservatives Like Regulation and Liberals Like Markets

We should distinguish carefully skepticism about big
government from contempt for all government.

—MITCH DANIELS

Contrary to popular belief, conservatives like regulation and liberals like markets. I know this may seem absurd. We are a politically divided nation. We live in blue states and red states. We watch Fox News or MSNBC. (People who watch both are trying to figure out what the enemy thinks.) We have competing notions of key concepts like liberty, equality, and democracy. We trust government or we mistrust it. We abhor compromise. If you watch the news, read the blogs, and follow the politics in Washington, D.C., you might well conclude that we are hopelessly deadlocked and committed to competing visions of where to go as a society and how to fix what is broken. Nor are these divisions only between Republicans and Democrats. The Tea Party radicals famously contend with mainstream Republicans. More quietly, but no less vigorously, liberals who want greater changes contend with pragmatists in the Democratic Party who counsel doing the best we can given divided power.

Despite all this evidence to the contrary, I want to swim upstream and argue that we are not as divided as it appears. There are core areas of agreement shared by conservatives and liberals alike, and those areas are far broader and more fundamental than we may realize. As the *American Prospect* noted:

> For many decades, political scientists have known that as a group, Americans are "symbolic conservatives" but "operational liberals." They like the idea of "small government," as long as you're staying at that level of abstraction. But they also like—and want to spend more on—just about everything government does.[1]

This observation is true not only about federal spending. It is true about American attitudes to "regulation." Americans hate "regulation" in the abstract, but when asked about particular regulatory laws they change their tune. Americans want consumer protection law; they want environmental laws that promote clean air and water; they want antidiscrimination laws; they want financial regulations that protect our money in the bank; they want laws that regulate eviction and foreclosure to protect us from being thrown on the street at a moment's notice.

I do not mean to ignore the clear facts about political discord or our obvious differences of opinion about the federal budget and taxation and regulatory issues. I do mean to point out that underlying these laws are value judgments, and our heated rhetoric has blinded us to the values we hold in common. We do not agree upon everything. But we do agree about some things, and the things we agree upon matter.

Conservatives and liberals alike are democrats with a small "d." That means we believe in liberty, equality, and democracy. Although there are large differences among us on what these values mean, we share a common understanding about some core values.

We want liberty. We have basic rights to "life, liberty, and the pursuit of happiness." That means we are empowered to choose how to live our lives as long as what we do is compatible with similar freedoms for others. We do not have an established religion; we have freedom of speech and conscience; and we enable individuals to choose where to live and how to live within limits established by law.

We want equality. Each person is "created equal." That means each person is equally important and equally free to enjoy liberty and security. There are no lords in America, no titles of nobility, no castes, no racial hierarchies. We have equal liberty to pursue happiness, and across the political spectrum we believe in the idea of equal opportunity. We may differ about what that means exactly, but it is not an empty concept; it has consequences for public policy and law.

We want democracy. We favor "government of the people, by the people, and for the people." Our constitution requires the states to have a "republican form of government." That means we use democratic means to choose our leaders and to shape the laws that set the ground rules for our interactions with each other. It means we develop political institutions and procedures to adjudicate conflicts and to agree upon laws that shape the environment within which we exercise our freedoms. We want collective power over lawmakers, but we also want the collective power to pass laws to define the contexts within which we exercise our liberties.

All this means we embrace democracy and the rule of law. I have explained that "regulation" is another word for "the rule of law." And that means that conservatives, libertarians, and liberals alike want regulation. We don't want stupid regulations or overly intrusive ones. What we want are rules of the game that ensure that we can participate in social and economic life in dignity. We want not anarchy but liberty—the kind of liberty enjoyed by citizens of a democracy. We want *democratic liberty*.

Understanding the ways in which law supports and shapes economic, social, and political institutions favored by conservatives and liberals alike will help us frame issues in a more productive manner. It will allow all of us to better understand and express our views while opening paths for potential agreement that would otherwise be obscured. Rather than arguing about *whether* to regulate the free market or to respect private property, we should focus on figuring out *what laws are needed* to establish minimum standards for market and property relationships compatible with the values of a free and democratic society. What rules ensure that hard work pays off and that every person—and that means every person—has an equal opportunity to live with dignity? What laws promote the free-doms characteristic of a democratic society?

How Regulation Promotes Conservative Values

Conservative rhetoric relentlessly attacks the very idea of "regu-lation." That is because laws that limit our freedom of action appear to take away our liberty, prevent us from entering con-tracts on terms we might want to choose, and limit what we can do with our property. Framed in that manner, "regulations" both violate our rights and impede social welfare. They violate our rights by taking away our freedom to pursue happiness in our own way, and they impede social welfare by interfering with the operation of free markets that allow efficient satisfaction of preferences and creation of wealth and prosperity.

Conservatives are completely correct to emphasize the value of individual freedom, markets, private property, and the laws that support them. The American idea that some truths are self-evident and that among them are "life, liberty, and the pursuit of happiness" is one of the great achievements of civilization. It celebrates the transition from a hierarchical, status-based, quasi-feudal system based on lords and common-ers and state monopolies to our modern democratic market system that abhors titles of nobility and promotes equal oppor-tunity. But conservatives are wrong to imply that all regulations represent an attack on liberty, free markets, and property. Indeed, as I have shown, our cherished liberties could not exist without regulation.

In some sense, conservatives realize this. For one thing, calls for "deregulation" tend to oppose new regulations and to cut back on or streamline existing ones. Almost no one calls for complete deregulation. No one is clamoring to get rid of all building codes, all zoning laws, all environmental laws, all banking and insurance laws, all workplace safety laws, or all antidiscrimination laws. We may fight about whether existing regulations are overly intrusive or necessary, and we may fight about proposals for new regulations. But no one wants to get rid of the laws that enable both markets and property to exist.

If we consider the substance of conservative arguments against regulation, we find that, when conservatives rally against regulation, they also assume that a lot of regulation will stay in place. That is not necessarily hypocritical, but it is a misleading picture of what conservatives are actually for. Conservative rhetoric is more extreme than conservative values. That is what is problematic about conservative rhetoric. It may inhibit both conservatives and liberals from recognizing how much regulation conservatives actually do support. If conservatives were more aware of their underlying assumptions about the benefits of the regulations we have (at least the good ones), then debate about current issues of the regulatory state could proceed on terms that might not only be more rational but have the possibility of attracting support from liberals as well.

Conservatives may not appreciate how much law is necessary to achieve their own values. They may also not recognize how seemingly "liberal" laws actually achieve conservative ends. Most regulations supported by liberals serve four purposes: they ensure equal opportunity; they protect consumers; they create the necessary legal infrastructure for property; and they protect us from harmful externalities caused by the actions of others. What is striking about each of these purposes is that each one of them is a conservative purpose.

We generally think of conservatives as championing liberty while it is liberals who champion equality. But that is a mistake. Conservatives favor equality as liberals do; they simply interpret what it means differently. Consider that conservatives of any stripe would not be happy if New Jersey were still owned by two lords who not only owned the land but ruled it. Conservatives may oppose "redistribution," but that is because they forget that redistribution was necessary to wrest property away from lords and democratize it, giving the people the power to become lords of their own castles. Conservatives do not like redistribution because they believe owners earned their property. But that belief assumes that our system has made it possible for anyone to become an owner and to live a comfortable life. It assumes that anyone who works hard will earn what they deserve.

Both conservatives and liberals accept the value of equal opportunity. No one thinks we should have fixed statuses, titles of nobility, slavery, limited opportunities for women, racial segregation or discrimination, classes, or castes. While we usually think of equal opportunity as the core conservative value, and equal outcomes as a liberal goal, the truth of the matter is that equal opportunity is as much a liberal as a conservative value and no one (including liberals) is in favor of the draconian laws that would be necessary to ensure absolutely equal outcomes.

Liberals take unequal outcomes to be a sign that equal opportunity is missing. Conservatives are more likely to assume that equal opportunity already exists. Both camps think that each person is created equal and has an equal right to pursue happiness and that our laws should make it realistically possible for each person to succeed and have a dignified, comfortable life.

Our disagreements seem to be about the facts, not about the value of equal opportunity itself. Of course, factual disagreements also are disagreements about how to interpret what equal opportunity means. Conservatives assume that existing institutions already make it possible for any person to succeed, while liberals think there are social, familial, educational, racial, and other barriers to equal opportunity.[2] We do not agree, then, on exactly what the value of equal opportunity is. At the same time, laws intended to promote equal opportunity, such as antidiscrimination laws, can be supported by conservatives as much as by liberals. Disagreement comes with laws like minimum wage laws, where there are differences about whether such laws help or hurt working Americans. Conservatives view the evidence one way and liberals the other. But there is a core agreement that the underlying normative goal is equal opportunity to participate in economic life, and that core agreement could help channel discussion in a more fruitful manner.

Consumer protection laws, as I have explained, ensure that consumers get what they want out of contracts. Far from regulations that limit our choices or interfere with our freedom, such laws promote freedom of contract by preventing sellers from cheating us and instead forcing sellers to give us what we wanted out of the agreement. Some of these laws set default terms for contracts by defining what ambiguous agreements will mean unless the parties contract to the contrary. Others set mandatory terms for agreements. Again, far from limiting our freedom, those mandatory terms laws are intended to ensure that we get what we want rather than stop us from contracting for what we want.

Some mandatory terms laws ensure that consumers get what they actually expect rather than what the written terms of the contract say. Freedom of contract does not mean slavish adherence to written forms; rather, it means deferring to the will of the parties. When the seller wants something different from what the buyer wants (and hides that fact in a long contract the buyer will not read and would not understand if she did read it), consumer protection laws favor the consumer. Although such a situation may prevent the seller from getting what it wants, it does not violate freedom of contract principles. That is because what the seller wants is illegitimate; the seller wants the buyer to think the contract means one thing while getting the buyer to agree to terms that are quite another thing. The name for this is cheating or theft or fraud, and it is a violation of both freedom of contract and property rights, as well as of consumer protection laws prohibiting unfair or deceptive conduct.

Harry Potter taught us about the concept of the "binding magical contract." Luckily for us, U.S. law does not enforce the written terms of agreements come hell or high water, no matter what they say. The law judges whether the written terms are what most people would think the contract was actually about and whether the contract reflects the likely wishes and goals of consumers.

Consumer protection law sometimes reflects our long-term goals rather than our short-term ones. We created Social Security because we know we should save for retirement, but we have a tendency to spend all our money in the moment. So we force ourselves to save to enable us to achieve our long-run goals, while in the short term it may feel like an interference with our freedom. But it actually promotes our freedom because we chose to enact the Social Security law. We could repeal the law; indeed, some have proposed doing exactly that. But the American people like Social Security; they want it. To conceptualize the Social Security law as taking away our freedom ignores the fact that we exercised our freedom in choosing to pass the law, and we continue to exercise our freedom by keeping it in place.

Consumer protection laws may be thought to make transactions more expensive because they ensure that products are safe, but those laws are ones we want. We know we have a tendency to buy the cheapest product and that cheaper may mean more dangerous. That is why we want laws that regulate the safety of consumer goods, drugs, and food, and laws that prevent pollution. We want to be protected from our own tendency to pick the cheapest product by choosing laws that set minimum standards for those products. All this means that consumer protection laws generally promote freedom of contract rather than interfere with it.

Regulatory laws also set the legal infrastructure for markets and private property. Conservatives are against force and fraud, and that is why they favor consumer protection laws that prevent deceptive conduct in business transactions. Subprime mortgages were marketed with mixed messages that effectively misled both borrowers and investors about the qualities of the mortgages they were selling or buying. Laws that prevent fraud and deception in the marketplace set the rules that determine which contracts are ones that can be enforced and which constitute double-dealing and rip-offs. As I have noted, consumer protection laws ensure that the written terms of form contracts are ignored and the consumers' actual expectations honored. And the law of contract remedies ensures both that there are incentives not to breach contracts and that people have the legitimate freedom to change their minds. We have no binding magical contracts that prevent people from quitting a job they hate or that force people to comply with terms we have defined as illegal. Laws about contract remedies make such judgments to ensure that we have the right mix of freedom of action and security.

Similarly, a great deal of law is necessary to have a private property system. I have shown how regulations are needed to have clear, public real estate titles to define the rights of owners; ensure access to public accommodations without regard to race, sex, or disability; adjudicate boundary disputes; allow orderly eviction but not allow landlords to change the locks and throw your stuff on the street without a hearing; ensure that condominium rules are not unreasonable; ensure that married couples share property on death or divorce; and protect the rights of tenants to have a working furnace in the winter. I could go on, and in my property law course I do go on. Property is complex, and a legal system that recognizes private property needs a lot of law to work properly. A lot of "regulation" that might be thought of as "liberal" actually is necessary to have a functioning private property system.

Finally, regulatory laws prevent us from harming others except in ways that are acceptable. The law does not prevent all harm. I am allowed to build a house on my property in accordance with the zoning law even if that interferes with your view. I am allowed to compete with your company even if it puts you out of business. I am allowed to drive sixty-five mph on the highway even if you would be safer if I drove thirty-five mph. But the law does prevent me from harming you in other ways. Negligence law requires me to act reasonably to protect you from foreseeable harms to your body or your property. Contract law requires me to act in good faith to comply with my legitimate contractual commitments. Property law prevents me from causing a nuisance that interferes with your quiet enjoyment of your property or which violates the zoning law or environmental law. Conservatives are not against laws that protect us from harm. Indeed, the protection of the individual is the core conservative norm.

The subprime crisis, more than anything else in recent history, shows that property rights affect not only those who are party to the transaction that created them. The subprime market created toxic assets that wrecked the world economy, and regulations are essential to avoid a repetition of this disaster. Such regulations do not interfere with freedom or markets or property; they promote all three by enabling our private property and free market systems to work well while protecting the freedom of owners to enjoy what they own.

It is true that we have sharp disagreements between Republicans and Democrats over the wisdom of various regulatory laws. These conflicts distract us from an underlying truth: Across the political spectrum we favor laws designed to support legitimate property rights and fair market relationships. When conservatives want regulation, they call it "protecting property rights" or "preventing fraud." They are right about this. Regulatory laws that serve legitimate purposes do protect our justified expectations by setting fair rules of the game. And that is what liberals mean when they argue for "regulation" of "the market." Again, we do not and will not agree upon everything, especially how to define what contracts are fair and just. But one thing is certain: A free and democratic society empowers individuals to pursue happiness, and that can happen only if we have a legal framework to ensure the freedom of each is compatible with the freedom of all. Democratic liberty requires democratic lawmaking. This is something conservatives and liberals should find they have in common.

Why Liberals Like Markets and Private Property

I have argued that regulation is necessary for freedom and that equality is a conservative value. Those arguments are directed at conservatives or libertarians who disparage government without appreciating the extent to which it promotes their values, including free markets and private property. It also reminds them how committed they are to the equal status of all persons and to the ideal of equal opportunity. But this argument is also directed toward liberals who are defensive about the government regulations they favor. I have tried to explain why regulation promotes freedom and protects property rights; liberals need not be wary of their legitimate instincts in favor of regulation. At the same time, I have explained that liberal values can often be justified through conservative arguments because regulation often promotes both the free market and private property. I have also argued that history can help remind conservatives about the regulations that were needed to create the freedoms we all cherish. Liberals, it turns out, can learn a great deal from that same historical lesson. What liberals would learn is the importance not of regulation but of both free markets and private property.

The conservative attack on regulation is understandable in the context of specific laws that conservatives oppose and in light of a general approach to politics, law, and social life. It is based on a vivid exemplar that is often not explicit. That exemplar is the premodern era, before modern capitalism, when government created monopolistic corporations, guilds limited entry into the professions, indentured servitude was widespread, and people were forever constrained by the class into which they were born, whether nobility or commoner or peasant. When we understand that the conservative love of freedom is based on opposition to those oppressive social institutions, we can see that liberals oppose those institutions as much as conservatives do. If deregulation means freedom from monopolies, guilds, indentured servitude, and ascribed status, then it is evident that liberals want deregulation as much as conservatives do.

There is a tendency for liberals to denigrate the free market because they see it as a mechanism that allows the strong to oppress the weak, or the rich to oppress the poor. Liberals also have a tendency to understand property rights as a code word for preserving inequality. It is easy for liberals to understand how regulation promotes equality, but it is harder for them to remember the ways in which both free markets and private property can promote both autonomy and equality.

Liberals are correct to presume that what is needed is an appropriate regulatory structure for both markets and property. But once we accept that these things cannot exist without a legal infrastructure, it becomes clear that both free markets and private property, properly structured, advance liberal values. Indeed, liberal values cannot be advanced without markets and private property. If liberals can understand this, they will realize they share more of the values of conservatives than they ever dreamed they did.

Liberals share most of the core values advanced by conservatives, especially including freedom, equality, and democracy. But liberals tend to leave free markets and property off their list of fundamental norms. They do so partly because they think that both markets and property are not rights or values in themselves; rather, they exist to promote other core values, such as freedom and security. However, liberals leave markets and property off the list for a more fundamental reason. They are well aware of the ways in which the concepts of "the free market" and "private property" have been used to protect the rights of the rich while leaving the poor vulnerable. Those concepts have also been used to promote the interests of employers against employees, developers against environmentalists, businesses against the public, and "profits" over "people."

I have no criticism of the liberal presumption that power is a problem and that private power, exercised through markets and property rights, is as much a danger as public power exercised by state officials. But I do take issue with the tendency to therefore hypostasize both "the free market" and "private property" to represent a conservative or a libertarian social vision. Liberal ideals of liberty, equality, and democracy in fact rest on the institutional structures encompassed by free markets and private property.

Liberals are comfortable with government regulation because they know how it can promote equal opportunity and protect us from unfair and deceptive practices. They sympathize with those who have it rough through no fault of their own, and they believe that the religious values that prompt conservatives to contribute to charity are the same values that underlie the welfare state. At the same time, liberals value freedom of choice as strongly as do libertarians. They believe, with John Locke and John Stuart Mill, that each person should have freedom of conscience and religion and be at liberty to choose what kind of work to do and where to live.

What causes liberals to worry about markets and private property is that they seem to protect the rights of those who have while leaving the have-nots out in the cold. If property is about keeping what you have and being entitled to exclude others, then it appears to benefit only the rich. If free markets are characterized by laissez-faire and caveat emptor, then subprime mortgages can flourish, and low-income families can be cheated out of their hard-earned dollars.

What liberals need to understand is that neither private property nor the free market has a built-in structure. Rather, there are multiple ways to define the rules of the road for markets and multiple ways to define, allocate, and regulate the packages of property rights that people have. Indeed, if we remember our history of rebellion against feudalism and our hard-won victory over the institutions of slavery and racial segregation and patriarchal privilege, it becomes clear that our property system has, over time, moved closer to the liberal ideal where each person is secure, free, comfortable. Not that we have solved all problems—the subprime crisis and the recent increases in both poverty and inequality are testaments to that. But what we have learned is that property is a system as well as an individual entitlement, and property systems can be legally structured to promote equal opportunity, widespread home ownership, a living wage, and ample employment.

So too with free markets; the ability to live where we like, to start our own businesses, to choose what kind of work to do and who to work for or with—all reflect liberal values of autonomy and equality. The free market does not limit participation to a particular caste or race or sex; it is regulated to make entry available without regard to invidious discrimination. Free markets do not mean no unions. Although conservatives see unions as interfering with free choice, liberals are justified in viewing them as a means of exercising freedom by associating with others for mutual advantage. Just as shareholders join hands to form a corporation, workers join hands to form a union. Requiring employers to negotiate with unions is not an interference with "the free market." Rather, it promotes freedom by giving workers the same rights to band together as shareholders enjoy.

The freedoms that liberals cherish are threatened not by free markets and private property in the abstract, but by particular institutional structures that favor the strong over the weak, the owner over the nonowner, the employer over the employee. The freedoms that liberals cherish would be enhanced, rather than impeded, by properly structured markets. Once we recall that the word "free" does not mean "no law" or "unregulated," then liberals can embrace free markets as warmly as libertarians. "Free markets" imply that they are subject to rules of the game, and those rules reflect democratic values that promote equal opportunity and protection from fraudulent and deceptive practices. I have argued that markets are not "free" without consumer protection laws in place. If liberals understand that there are no free markets without law and that "freedom" entails freedom from deception and abuse, then it becomes clear that markets are not free unless they are also fair. For example, public accommodation laws prevent restaurants from excluding patrons based on race or religion; such regulations promote rather than undermine "free" markets. Free markets are not devoid of "regulation"; rather, they are defined by laws that set minimum standards for market relationships. If liberals understand that markets are "free" because of laws that make them fair, they can embrace them.

There is no freedom without regulation, and that is true of free markets as well. Liberals are enemies not of free markets but of markets governed by unfair rules. Since markets cannot exist without rules, conservatives favor regulation as much as liberals do. And since freedom cannot exist without law, markets cannot be free unless they are fair. We should be debating what the minimum standards should be for free markets, not whether those regulations should exist at all. If we do that, then liberals can comfortably become champions of the free market while pressing for fair rules of the game. Liberals can also bring to light the implicit regulations favored by conservatives and try to show why those favored by liberals are more fair and thus better promote freedom.

Liberals also should realize that they are champions of private property. Like conservatives, they abhor feudalism and slavery. Like conservatives, they do not want all the property to be in the hands of the few. Liberals would do well to listen to Robert Montgomery, a liberal economist who was called before the Texas legislature during the McCarthy era to defend his views. He was asked if he favored private property and he answered by saying, "Yes I do, so much so that I want everyone in Texas to have some."

Liberals may be more insistent on correcting injustices in property distribution than conservatives, but that is because they have a different view about what type of distribution is necessary to prevent undue concentrations of power and to ensure equal opportunity. Liberals should recognize that a property system in a free and democratic society assumes that ownership is widespread and that anyone can become an owner. Accomplishing those goals, as we have seen, requires regulation. But this does not mean liberals do not like private property. It means that we need to figure out what regulations and policies need to be in place to make it true that each and every person has access to the institution of private property on terms that are meaningful and fair. Liberals are right to remind conservatives that regulation is needed to structure markets appropriately and to define property rights, but conservatives are right to remind liberals that the best way to promote equality is by those properly structured markets and property rights.

6

Democratic Liberty

> Whenever a separation is made between liberty and justice,
> neither, in my opinion, is safe.
>
> —EDMUND BURKE

"Where there is no Law," John Locke tells us, "there is no Freedom."[1] Freedom requires regulation, and free markets work only because they are structured by law. Libertarian ideals can be achieved only by a robust regulatory state. Conversely, liberal ideals of freedom and equality can be achieved only by a free economy that ensures equal opportunity to pursue happiness and to obtain property. Despite the current polarized state of political discourse, Americans agree upon a lot more than one might think. Surprisingly, Americans are also a lot more liberal than common wisdom recognizes. When it comes to government regulation, Americans talk like libertarians and legislate like liberals.

Of course, this leaves a very wide range of possible disagreement between the two camps. But if the subprime crisis teaches us anything, it is that free markets require law to work properly. Such laws do not infringe on liberty; law makes liberty possible. The laws of property in particular have profound effects on both civil rights and civil liberties, and those freedoms can be protected and promoted only by suitable regulations. Liberty entails not only freedom from unwarranted government restrictions on how we live but adequate government restraints that enable us to live peaceably with others in a setting of mutual concern and respect.

Laws promote both freedom and democracy by outlawing social and economic relationships that are "subprime" because they fall below the minimum standards of a free and democratic society. We regulate the terms of contracts and the rights associated with property in order to ensure that we can retain adequate independence and freedom while remaining secure from undue interference by others. We obtain security only by limiting freedom of action; that means that liberty cannot be furthered by eliminating government "regulation."

We have outlawed feudalism, titles of nobility, slavery, male privileges, racial segregation, and discriminatory denial of access to the market. These laws limit the contracts we can enter and the property rights we can create, but they do not take away our freedom; they define what it means to live in a free society that treats each person with dignity. And we have demanded and promulgated myriad consumer protection and other regulatory laws to ensure that we can enter the marketplace protected by a set of rules that allows us to bargain from a position of safety and security. Those laws also protect our liberty by ensuring that we get what we want when we enter the marketplace.

We demand laws that allow us to take certain things for granted, to free us from having to bargain for them. We seek law not because we are irrational or weak and not because we do not value liberty. We seek law because we demand to be treated like human beings and we seek to be treated by others as they would want to be treated. We seek law because people should not take unfair advantage of others. We seek a legal infrastructure that frees us to pursue our dreams in safety and harmony. The subprime crisis is an occasion to remember that the American ideals of equality and liberty require laws that regulate market transactions to ensure that we are free from unfair practices and that our economic system is not periodically threatened by the negligent creation of toxic assets. The subprime crisis should remind us that equal opportunity and equal access to the American dream require a legal infrastructure that properly channels markets and fairly allocates and protects property rights.

I have a button that was given to me by someone who loves me and knows me well. It says: "stubbornly clinging to utopian illusions." Well, that's me. Don't get me wrong. I don't expect conflict or disagreement to go away; I don't expect harmony or convergence. But I am enough of an optimist and enough of a scholar to believe that examining our beliefs can enable us to take a step in the direction of greater mutual understanding.

It will help if conservatives reflect on what is great about regulation or, as I prefer to call it, "democracy" and "the rule of law." It will help if liberals reflect on what is great about free markets and private property and what is worrisome about "government regulation." And both liberals and conservatives would better advance their own values if we recognized that markets, like games, have rules. The question is what fair rules of the game look like, not whether to have rules at all.

In his satirical novel *Jennifer Government,* Max Barry describes a libertarian dystopia where deregulation has run amok.[2] The government has been privatized and people get the police protection they are willing and able to pay for. There are no limits on freedom of contract, and written contracts are enforced to the letter—no matter what they say. Contracting parties are free to hire either private or public agents to enforce the terms of those contracts.

The book begins when the hero signs an employment contract without reading it. Bad move. That contract was dreamed up by the marketing department of his company, which believes that the company could sell more sneakers if consumers thought the sneakers were so cool that people were willing to die to get a pair. The marketers drum up demand for the sneakers by severely limiting the supply until their customers are chomping at the bit. The marketers then dupe the hapless hero into signing a contract that requires him to kill a few customers as they cluster around the store waiting for it to open. The whole idea is to make the shoes cool and increase demand for them. Because our hero has already signed the contract, he is bound by its penalties if he fails to perform, and those penalties demand more than a pound of flesh.

Although in Barry's parallel universe killing is technically illegal, enforcement occurs only through private initiative, depending on private demand. Moreover, the company would only have to pay a fine for breaking this law. This is thought to promote economic efficiency; the law against murder should be broken if the company is willing to pay more to violate it than what others would to enforce it. The hero also can get help from the police to protect him from contract enforcement by the company if he is willing and able to pay the police enough to induce them to protect him from the company. The police will aid the family of a murder victim in finding the murderer only if the family is willing and able to hire them to do so. Everything has a price, and the rule of law is no different; you get the police protection you can afford. The marketers of course choose poor victims to kill; their families will be no threat because they cannot afford police protection. At the climax of the novel, the marketing director decides that it is time to be free from all intrusive government regulation—and that means *all*. The company issues a declaration of independence, freeing the corporation from government regulation entirely. But no rules means no rules, and economic competition slides inexorably into war.

It is all an implausible romp, I suppose, but Barry's novel is meant to prove a point: freedom without law is not liberty, and the free market without a legal structure is not a market in any sense we would recognize. This means that liberty is not possible without regulation; paradoxically, the liberty we experience in the private sphere is possible only because of the regulation we impose in the public sphere. Indeed, it is fair to say that when we talk about liberty, we are talking about the benefits of living within a just regulatory structure.

Neither the free market nor private property can function without law. Law establishes minimum standards for economic and social relationships compatible with the norms and values of a free and democratic society. Arrangements that do not meet these minimum standards are *subprime,* and for that reason they are out of bounds. Laws prohibiting subprime arrangements do not take away our freedom; they guarantee it. When they are adopted through appropriate procedures, and when they reflect our deepest values, they promote democratic liberty. It is time we acknowledged the regulations we too often take for granted. If we do that, we can debate what those laws should be, rather than focusing on a false debate about whether they should exist at all.

Notes

1.
The Subprime Challenge

1. This joke won second place in an online contest to find the funniest joke. See Geoff Anandappa, *In second place*, LAUGHLAB.CO.UK, http://www.richardwiseman.com/LaughLab/second.html (last visited June 29, 2011).

2. Eric Scheiner, *Ted Cruz: 49 Reasons to Stop Obamacare*, cnsnews. com, http://cnsnews.com/mrctv-blog/eric-scheiner/ted-cruz-49-reasons-stop-obamacare.

3. *Id.*

4. CHARLES MURRAY, WHAT IT MEANS TO BE A LIBERTARIAN: A PERSONAL INTERPRETATION 38 (1997) ("Strict protection against force or fraud"); *id.* at 27–29 (protect property rights).

5. *Greenspan Admits "Flaw" to Congress, Predicts More Economic Problems*, http://www.pbs.org/newshour/bb/business/july-dec08/crisishearing_10–23.html; see also http://www.youtube.com/watch?v=DqeoVqIOrFQ.

6. *Id.*

7. *Id.*

8. JOSEPH E. STIGLITZ, FREEFALL: AMERICA, FREE MARKETS, AND THE SINKING OF THE WORLD ECONOMY xii (2010).

9. William Echikson, *Euphoria Dies Down in Czechoslovakia*, WALL ST. J., Sept. 18, 1990, at A26.

10. One of the most important libertarian philosophers who does seem to realize the complications involved in setting rules for markets and property systems is Friedrich Hayek. *See* FRIEDRICH A. HAYEK, THE CONSTITUTION OF LIBERTY (1960).

11. The legal realists demolished this myth a century ago in their scholarly works. *See, e.g.,* Morris Cohen, *The Basis of Contract*, 46 HARV. L. REV. 553 (1933); Morris Cohen, *Property and Sovereignty*, 13 CORNELL

L. Q. 8 (1927); Walter Wheeler Cook, *Privileges of Labor Unions in the Struggle for Life*, 27 YALE L. J. 779 (1918); Robert Hale, *Bargaining, Duress, and Economic Liberty*, 43 COLUM. L. REV. 603 (1943); Robert Hale, *Coercion and Distribution in a Supposedly Non-Coercive State*, 38 POL. SCI. Q. 470 (1923); Roscoe Pound, *Liberty of Contract*, 18 YALE L. J. 454 (1909). *See generally* Joseph William Singer, *Legal Realism Now*, 76 CALIF. L. REV. 465 (1988).

12. Former Republican Whip Eric Cantor criticized the new financial regulation law by arguing that "[t]his legislation is a clear attack on capital formation in America. It purports to prevent the next financial crisis, but it does so by vastly expanding the power of the same regulators who failed to prevent the last one." Representative John Boehner said that the financial regulation law was like "killing an ant with a nuclear weapon." David H. Herszenhorn, *Finance Overhaul Approved by House*, N.Y. TIMES, July 1, 2010, http://query.nytimes.com/gst/fullpage.html?res=9D04EEDB1F3CF932A35754C0A9669D8B63&scp=4&sq=herszenhorn%20finance%20overhaul&st=Search.

13. Binyamin Appelbaum, *Expansion of Mortgage Program Is Limited in Scope*, N.Y. TIMES, Oct. 24, 2011, http://www.nytimes.com/2011/10/25/us/politics/administration-proposes-changes-to-mortgage-refinancing-program.html?_r=1&scp=1&sq=romney%20free%20market&st=cse.

14. I will speak about libertarians and conservatives interchangeably here not because all conservatives are libertarians but because the groups overlap when it comes to economic policy. Libertarians want deregulation of both economic life and personal (including sexual) life while conservatives are libertarian when it comes to economics but in favor of regulation when it comes to sexuality. Because my focus is economics (markets and property), I am analyzing the libertarians' views of both groups. Because conservatives outnumber libertarians, I will generally use the term "conservative" to signify that my argument applies to them as well as to doctrinaire libertarians.

15. JOHN LOCKE, THE SECOND TREATISE OF GOVERNMENT ¶ 57, at 306 (Peter Laslett ed., 1988, Cambridge Univ. Press, 2009 reprinting) (original 1690) (italics in original).

16. Matt Bai, *Establishment Republicans Look at These Guys and Say "You're Nuts!": The G.O.P. Elite Tries to Take Its Party Back*, N.Y. TIMES MAGAZINE, Oct. 16, 2011, at 45, 50.

17. Peggy Noonan, *Declarations: Republicans Break the Ice,* WALL ST. J., Feb. 2, 2013, at A–15.

18. *See* SUSAN NEIMAN, MORAL CLARITY: A GUIDE FOR GROWN-UP IDEALISTS (2008).

19. JEREMY BENTHAM, 1 THEORY OF LEGISLATION 139 (1840).

20. For an example of libertarian thinkers who vastly underestimate the difficulty of defining and operating a private property system, see DAVID BOAZ, LIBERTARIANISM: A PRIMER 68–74, 154–156 (1997) (arguing for the protection of "property rights" without discussion of their meaning, interpretation, or limits); CHARLES MURRAY, WHAT IT MEANS TO BE A LIBERTARIAN: A PERSONAL INTERPRETATION 27–29 (1997) (arguing for the protection of property rights but with little elaboration, suggesting that interpreting what that means is a simple business).

21. Libertarians tend to conceptualize fraud as a form of theft. *See* DAVID BOAZ, LIBERTARIANISM: A PRIMER 75 (1997) ("fraud is a form of theft").

2.
Why a Free and Democratic Society Needs Law

1. LEVIATHAN (C. B. MacPherson ed., Penguin Classics 1968) (original 1651); JOHN LOCKE, THE SECOND TREATISE OF GOVERNMENT (Peter Laslett ed., 1988, Cambridge Univ. Press, 2009 reprinting) (original 1690).

2. THOMAS HOBBES, LEVIATHAN (C.B. MacPherson ed., Penguin Classics 1968) (original 1651); JOHN LOCKE, THE SECOND TREATISE OF GOVERNMENT ¶ 57, at 306 (Peter Laslett ed., 1988, Cambridge Univ. Press, 2009 reprinting) (original 1690) (italics in original).

3. For qualified defenses of the idea of first possession as the origin of property, see Richard A. Epstein, *Possession as the Root of Title,* 13 GA. L. REV. 1221 (1979); James E. Krier, *Evolutionary Theory and the Origin of Property Rights,* 95 CORNELL L. REV. 139 (2009); Carol M. Rose, *Possession as the Origin of Property,* 52 U. CHI L. REV. 73 (1985). For a critique of this view, see Joseph William Singer, *Original Acquisition of Property: From Conquest and Possession to Democracy and Equal Opportunity,* 86 IND. L. J. 1 (2011).

4. Pierson v. Post, 2 Am. Dec. 264 (N.Y. 1805).

5. Harold Demsetz, *Toward a Theory of Property Rights,* 57 AM. ECON. REV. 347, 354–358 (1967).

6. For accounts of this history, see FRANK BARLOW, THE FEUDAL KINGDOM OF ENGLAND, 1042–1216 (5th ed. 1999); DAVID CARPENTER, THE STRUGGLE FOR MASTERY: THE PENGUIN HISTORY OF BRITAIN, 1066–1284 (2003); RICHARD HUSCROFT, RULING ENGLAND, 1042–1217 (2005); EDMUND KING, MEDIEVAL ENGLAND FROM HASTINGS TO BOSWORTH (2009). *See also* IAN MORTIMER, THE TIME TRAVELER'S GUIDE TO MEDIEVAL ENGLAND: A HANDBOOK FOR VISITORS TO THE FOURTEENTH CENTURY 36–59 (2008) (explaining social relationships in the 1300s).

7. *See* DAVID CARPENTER, THE STRUGGLE FOR MASTERY: THE PENGUIN HISTORY OF BRITAIN, 1066–1284, at 84–87, 392–430 (2003) (describing structures of society in early feudal practice in England).

8. DAVID CARPENTER, THE STRUGGLE FOR MASTERY: THE PENGUIN HISTORY OF BRITAIN, 1066–1284, at 84–85, 403–406 (2003) (describing the practice of fealty).

9. On the role of women in this period, see DAVID CARPENTER, THE STRUGGLE FOR MASTERY: THE PENGUIN HISTORY OF BRITAIN, 1066–1284, at 415–422 (2003); IAN MORTIMER, THE TIME TRAVELER'S GUIDE TO MEDIEVAL ENGLAND: A HANDBOOK FOR VISITORS TO THE FOURTEENTH CENTURY 54–59 (2008).

10. *See* IAN MORTIMER, THE TIME TRAVELER'S GUIDE TO MEDIEVAL ENGLAND: A HANDBOOK FOR VISITORS TO THE FOURTEENTH CENTURY 39–59 (2008) (describing medieval social hierarchies).

11. For an excellent history, see A.W.B. SIMPSON, A HISTORY OF THE LAND LAW (2d ed. 1986).

12. RICHARD HUSCROFT, RULING ENGLAND, 1042–1217, at 176–187 (2005); EDMUND KING, MEDIEVAL ENGLAND FROM HASTINGS TO BOSWORTH 68–72 (2009).

13. BRENDAN MCCONVILLE, THOSE DARING DISTURBERS OF THE PUBLIC PEACE: THE STRUGGLE FOR PROPERTY AND POWER IN EARLY NEW JERSEY (1999); CHARLES W. MCCURDY, THE ANTI-RENT ERA IN NEW YORK LAW AND POLITICS, 1839–1865 (2001).

14. This response encapsulates a complicated history. For a summary, see BRENDAN MCCONVILLE, THOSE DARING DISTURBERS OF THE PUBLIC PEACE: THE STRUGGLE FOR PROPERTY AND POWER IN EARLY NEW JERSEY 12–27 (1999).

15. This version of the history is based on BRENDAN MCCONVILLE, THOSE DARING DISTURBERS OF THE PUBLIC PEACE: THE STRUGGLE FOR PROPERTY AND POWER IN EARLY NEW JERSEY 12–27 (1999). *See also* EDWIN P. TANNER, THE PROVINCE OF NEW JERSEY, 1664–1738 (1967).

16. CHARLES W. MCCURDY, THE ANTI-RENT ERA IN NEW YORK LAW AND POLITICS, 1839–1865, at 2 (Chapel Hill, N.C.: Univ. of N.C. Press 2001).

17. De Peyster v. Michael, 6 N.Y. 467 (1852).

18. *Id.* at 489.

19. *See* Claire Priest, *Creating an American Property Law: Alienability and Its Limits in American History*, 113 HARV L. REV. 1 (1999).

20. *Id.*

21. U.S. CONST. amend. 1.

22. THE DECLARATION OF INDEPENDENCE (1776).

23. U.S. CONST. art. I, § 9, cl. 8.

24. U.S. CONST. art. I, § 10, cl. 1 ("No state shall . . . grant any title of nobility"); U.S. CONST. art. IV, § 4 ("The United States shall guarantee to every state in this union a republican form of government . . .").

25. JOSEPH WILLIAM SINGER, PROPERTY § 9.2.2, at 396–397 (4th ed. 2014).

26. *Id.*, at § 2.6, at 47–79, §§ 12.1 to 12.8, at 581–632.

27. RESTATEMENT (SECOND) OF CONTRACTS § 367 (1981).

28. John B. Mitchell & Kelly Kunsch, *Access to Justice: Of Driver's Licenses and Debtor's Prison*, 4 SEATTLE J. SOC. JUST. 439, 444–446 (2005) (describing the abolition of debtor's prison). *But see* Elaine McArdle, *First Public Service Venture Fund "Seed Grant" Recipients Challenge Debtors' Prison in Alabama*, HARVARD LAW TODAY, June 13, 2014, http://today.law.harvard.edu/first-public-service-venture-fund-seed-grant-recipients-challenge-debtors-prison-alabama/.

29. This does not mean that tenants do not have obligations to landlords such as the duty not to commit waste or cause a nuisance to neighbors. JOSEPH WILLIAM SINGER, BETHANY R. BERGER, NESTOR M. DAVIDSON, & EDUARDO MOISÉS PEÑALVER, PROPERTY LAW: RULES, POLICIES, AND PRACTICES 335–366, 761–767 (6th ed. 2014).

30. State v. Shack, 277 A.2d 369, 374 (N.J. 1971); JOSEPH WILLIAM SINGER, PROPERTY § 2.2.2, at 31–32 (4th ed. 2014). Of course, the scope of the tenant's rights is indeed in contention. Landlords have, with some frequency, sought to exclude unmarried couples from their property. *See, e.g.*, McCready v. Hoffius, 586 N.W.2d 723 (Mich. 1998), *vacated and remanded*, 593 N.W.2d 545 (1999).

31. State v. Shack, 277 A.2d 369, 372 (N.J. 1971).

32. *Id.* at 374.

33. *Id.* at 374–375.

34. Adam Nagourney & Carl Hulse, *Tea Party Pick Causes Uproar on Civil Rights,* N.Y. TIMES, May 20, 2010, http://www.nytimes.com/2010/05/21/us/politics/21paul.html?scp=3&sq=rand%20paul%20civil%20rights&st=cse. *See also* CHARLES MURRAY, WHAT IT MEANS TO BE A LIBERTARIAN: A PERSONAL INTERPRETATION 38 (1997) (arguing for the complete abolition of all civil rights laws that prohibit discrimination by nongovernmental actors); *id* at 81–83 (arguing that freedom of association includes the freedom not to associate and that any laws mandating association interfere with personal liberty).

35. Of course, there are limits to this principle. Individuals are entitled, for example, to exercise their autonomy and associational freedom by giving gifts to specific individuals or limited groups; a prime example is the United Negro College Fund. This means that the principles of equal racial access must be defined by law and may be limited by competing principles and norms.

36. Joseph William Singer, *The Anti-Apartheid Principle in American Property Law,* 1 ALA. C.R.-C.L. L. REV. 91 (2011).

37. Associated Press, *Apartment Dweller, Managers Clash over Flag Display,* June 6, 2004, http://www.firstamendmentcenter.org/news.aspx?id=13469; *see also* Tony Mauro, *An Unwelcome Mat for Free Speech,* USA TODAY, Aug. 18, 2004, at 13A; Eric Olson, *Father-in-Law of High Court Justice Defies Rule, Flies Flag,* ST. LOUIS POST-DISPATCH, May 29, 2004, at 6.

38. Freedom to Display the American Flag Act of 2005, 4 U.S.C. § 5 note (Pub. L. 109–243, 120 Stat. 572, enacted July 24, 2006).

39. Robert Gordon, *Did Liberals Cause the Sub-Prime Crisis?* THE AMERICAN PROSPECT, Apr. 7, 2008, http://prospect.org/cs/articles?article=did_liberals_cause_the_subprime_crisis.

40. *Id.*

41. Of course, this period also witnessed widespread racial discrimination in the housing market, promoted not only by private actors but by both the federal and many state governments. The civil rights laws of the 1960s sought to extend property rights to previously excluded racial groups.

42. BETHANY MCLEAN & JOE NOCERA, ALL THE DEVILS ARE HERE: THE HIDDEN HISTORY OF THE FINANCIAL CRISIS 48–51 (2010); JOSEPH E. STIGLITZ, FREEFALL: AMERICA, FREE MARKETS, AND THE SINKING OF THE WORLD ECONOMY 10–11 (2010).

43. *See, e.g.,* David Abromowitz & Janneke Ratcliffe, *Homeownership Done Right: What Experience and Research Teaches Us,* CENTER FOR AMERICAN PROGRESS, Apr. 1, 2010, http://www.americanprogress.org/issues/2010/04/homeownership_right.html.

44. They are New Jersey, N.J. STAT. §§ 2A:18–61.1 to 2A:18–61.12, and the District of Columbia, D.C. CODE § 45–2551.

45. Congress did pass a temporary statute giving rent-paying tenants three extra months before they can be evicted from property when the owner loses title to foreclosure. *See* Protecting Tenants at Foreclosure Act, 12 U.S.C. § 5201 note, § 5220 note, 42 U.S.C. § 1437f(o)(7)(C) & (F), Pub. L. 111–22, 123. Stat. 1632, §§ 701–704. And Massachusetts passed a law prohibiting eviction of such tenants until title passes from the bank that bought the property at foreclosure to a third party. *See* Tenant Protections in Foreclosed Properties, MASS. GEN. LAWS ch. 186A, §§ 1–6.

46. ROBERT NOZICK, ANARCHY, STATE, AND UTOPIA 180 (1974) ("Thus a person may not appropriate the only water hole in a desert and charge what he will.").

47. For an explanation of how much law reform we would have to undertake if we took the principle of equal opportunity seriously, see BRIAN BARRY, WHY SOCIAL JUSTICE MATTERS (2005).

3.
Why Consumer Protection Promotes the Free Market

1. *Letter from Republican Senators to President Obama,* Feb. 1, 2013, http://big.assets.huffingtonpost.com/February2013Letterto PresidentObama.pdf.

2. *Letter from Democratic Senators to President Obama,* Feb. 14, 2013, http://www.banking.senate.gov/public/index.cfm?FuseAction= Files.View&FileStore_id=092ac137–38b3–48e5–9887–8fe7220c54fa. For arguments supporting this view, see Jennifer Bendery, *Richard Cordray CFPB Confirmation Imperiled by Senate Republicans,* HUFFINGTON POST, Feb. 1, 2013, http://www.huffingtonpost.com/2013/02/01/richard-cordray-cfpb_n_2599838.html; Jonathan Cohn, *The New Nullification: GOP v. Obama Nominees,* NEW REPUBLIC, July 19, 2011, http://www.newrepublic.com/blog/jonathan-cohn/92167/cordray-warren-cfpb-obama-republicans-nomination#; Andrew Rosenthal, *Republicans Versus Consumers,* N.Y. TIMES, Feb. 4, 2013, http://takingnote.blogs.

nytimes.com/2013/02/04/republicans-versus-consumers/?ref=cons
umerfinancialprotectionbureau. *See also* Adam J. Levitin, *Written
Testimony: Enhanced Consumer Financial Protection After the Financial
Crisis,* July 19, 2011, http://www.banking.senate.gov/public/index.
cfm?FuseAction=Files.View&FileStore_id=9c5cde82-c4b0–
4170–97c1–26aa872c1be3.

3. *Letter from Republican Senators to President Obama,* Feb. 1, 2013,
http://big.assets.huffingtonpost.com/February2013LettertoPresident
Obama.pdf.

4. Alan Schwartz, *Justice and the Law of Contracts: A Case for the
Traditional Approach,* 9 Harv. J. L. & Pub. Pol'y Rev. 110, 114–115 (1986).
See also N. Gregory Mankiw, *When the Scientist Is Also a Philosopher: In
Giving Policy Advice, Economists Are Also Making Their Own Political
Judgments,* N.Y. Times, Mar. 23, 2014, at Sunday Business Section, p. 4
("[W]e economists should be sure to apply the principle 'first, do no
harm.' . . . This principle suggests that when people have voluntarily
agreed upon an economic arrangement to their mutual benefit, that
arrangement should be respected. [The main exception is when
there are adverse effects on third parties—what economists call
'negative externalities.']").

5. *See* Christopher L. Peterson, *Predatory Structured Finance,* 28
Cardozo L. Rev. 90 (2007) (consumer protection law must be updated
to address the problems associated with predatory lending and
finance).

6. Joseph William Singer, *Subprime: Why a Free and Democratic
Society Needs Law,* 47 Harv. C.R.-C.L. L. Rev. 141, 155 n.45 (2012) (col-
lecting statutes).

7. 15 U.S.C. § 45.

8. David A. Fahrenthold, *Company Officials Had Worried About
Violations at Mine Before Explosion,* Wash. Post, Apr. 27, 2010, http://
www.washingtonpost.com/wp-dyn/content/article/2010/04/26/
AR2010042601770.html.

9. Charles Dickens, Oliver Twist (1838); Upton Sinclair, The
Jungle (1906).

10. *See, e.g.,* Idaho Code §§ 48–601 to 619 (Idaho Consumer
Protection Act).

11. *See, e.g.,* Idaho Code § 48–603 (prohibition against represent-
ing products to be safe when they are not); Idaho Code §§ 39–1601 to
1607 (regulating safety in food establishments).

12. *See, e.g.,* IDAHO CODE §§ 44–1401 to 1407 (making employers liable for harms to workers caused by unsafe workplace conditions).

13. *See, e.g.,* IDAHO CODE § 41–1402 (regulating insurance companies).

14. IDAHO CODE § 26–601 (regulating bank reserves).

15. *See, e.g.,* IDAHO CODE §§ 39–4101 to 4029 (regulating building construction).

16. *See, e.g.,* IDAHO CODE §§ 32–701 to 715 (regulating separate and community property on divorce).

17. *See, e.g.,* IDAHO CODE § 39–3601 to 3639 (Idaho Water Quality Act); IDAHO CODE §§ 67–6501 to 6538 (Idaho zoning enabling statute).

18. *See, e.g.,* IDAHO CODE § 18–7301 (prohibiting discrimination in employment and public accommodations).

19. *See, e.g.,* IDAHO CODE § 15–2–102 (prohibiting disinheritance of a spouse); IDAHO CODE § 18–7301 (prohibiting discrimination in employment and public accommodations); IDAHO CODE § 26–601 (regulating bank reserves); IDAHO CODE §§ 30–1–1620 to 1621 (mandating corporate disclosures of information to investors); IDAHO CODE § 39–1601 to 1607 (regulating safety in food establishments); IDAHO CODE §§ 39–4101 to 4029 (regulating building construction); IDAHO CODE § 41–1402 (regulating insurance companies); IDAHO CODE §§ 44–1401 to 1407 (making employers liable for harms to workers caused by unsafe workplace conditions); IDAHO CODE §§ 44–1501 to 1509 (requiring employers to pay minimum wages).

20. I am putting to one side a standard argument that sellers cannot pass on the added costs of new regulations if consumers refuse to pay higher prices for the goods. Limits on demand for goods may indeed inhibit the ability to pass on such costs. *See, e.g.,* Duncan Kennedy, *The Effect of the Warranty of Habitability on Low Income Housing: "Milking" and Class Violence,* 15 FLA. ST. L. REV. 485 (1987) (explaining why regulations may help consumers). My focus here is on how to justify regulations even if part or all of the cost is passed on to customers. And indeed, assuming there is a market for regulated products (i.e., sufficient demand to make providing the products profitable), then it is a truism that regulation may increase the cost of providing the product beyond what customers would have demanded or sellers would have provided in the absence of the regulatory requirement.

21. While some regulations merely set default terms that can be renegotiated by the parties, others represent judgments by lawmaking bodies (whether courts or legislatures) that certain minimum standards are required to ensure that each person is treated with respect and dignity. Such mandatory regulations do deprive individuals of the freedom to enter alternative arrangements, but they represent democratically adopted judgments that certain rights are too fundamental to be bargained away.

22. Edward M. Gramlich, *Booms and Busts: The Case of Subprime Mortgages,* THE URBAN INSTITUTE, 2007, http://www.urban.org/UploadedPDF/411542_Gramlich_final.pdf.

23. Securities and Exchange Act, 15 U.S.C. § 78j (unlawful to use any "manipulative or deceptive device or contrivance" in connection with the sale of any security); 17 C.F.R. § 240.10b–5 (unlawful, in connection with the sale of any security, to "defraud" or "to make any untrue statement of a material fact or to omit to state a material fact necessary in order to make the statements made, in light of the circumstances under which they were made, not misleading").

24. Joseph William Singer, *Subprime: Why a Free and Democratic Society Needs Law,* 47 HARV. C.R.-C.L. L. REV. 141, 157 (2012).

25. Commonwealth v. Fremont Investment & Loan, 897 N.E.2d 548, 558–559 (Mass. 2008); Joseph William Singer, *Property Law as the Infrastructure of Democracy* [The Fourth in the Wolf Family Lecture Series on the American Law of Real Property], 11–1 POWELL ON REAL PROPERTY (2011); Joseph William Singer, *Subprime: Why a Free and Democratic Society Needs Law,* 47 HARV. C.R.-C.L. L. REV. 141, 159 (2012).

26. 12 C.F.R. § 1026 (amending Regulation Z, implementing the Truth in Lending Act (TILA), 15 U.S.C. §§ 1639c, which itself implements the Mortgage Reform and Anti-Predatory Lending Act which constituted Title XIV of the Dodd-Frank Wall Street Reform and Consumer Protection Act, Pub. L. 111–203, H.R. 4173, July 21, 2010, at §§ 1411–1412). *See* Ability to Repay and Qualified Mortgage Standards Under the Truth in Lending Act (Regulation Z), http://www.consumerfinance.gov/regulations/ability-to-repay-and-qualified-mortgage-standards-under-the-truth-in-lending-act-regulation-z/; https://www.federalregister.gov/articles/2013/01/30/2013-00736/ability-to-repay-and-qualified-mortgage-standards-under-the-truth-in-lending-act-regulation-z.

27. DANIEL KAHNEMAN, THINKING, FAST AND SLOW (2011).

28. RICHARD H. THALER & CASS. R. SUNSTEIN, NUDGE: IMPROVING DECISIONS ABOUT HEALTH, WEALTH, AND HAPPINESS (2009).

29. John Cassidy, *After the Blowup: Laissez-Faire Economists Do Some Soul-Searching—and Finger-Pointing*, THE NEW YORKER, Jan. 11, 2010, at 28; RICHARD H. THALER & CASS SUNSTEIN, NUDGE (Penguin, 2009).

30. T. H. WHITE, THE ONCE AND FUTURE KING 381 (1939) (Ace ed. 1996).

4.
Why Private Property Needs a Legal Infrastructure

1. Stop the Beach Renourishment, Inc. v. Fla. Dep't of Envtl. Protection, 560 U.S. 702 (U.S. 2009).

2. Adam Nagourney, *Tiny Hawaiian Island Will See If New Owner Tilts at Windmills*, N.Y. TIMES, Aug. 23, 2012, at A1.

3. Kathleen Pender, *So What Did Ellison Buy in His Hawaiian Island?*, S.F. CHRON., June 27, 2012, at D1.

4. Richard A. Hawkins, *James D. Dole and the 1932 Failure of the Hawaiian Pineapple Company*, 41 HAW. J. HIST. 149, 149–50 (2007); Kathleen Pender, *So What Did Ellison Buy in His Hawaiian Island?*, S.F. CHRON., June 27, 2012, at D1.

5. Gary A. Warner, *Oracle's Billionaire CEO Purchases Hawaiian Island of Lanai*, VANCOUVER SUN, July 17, 2012, at B8.

6. *See* Joseph William Singer, *Subprime: Why a Free and Democratic Society Needs Law*, 47 HARV. C.R.-C.L. L. REV. 141 (2012).

7. People ex rel. Moloney v. Pullman's Palace-Car Co., 51 N.E. 664, 674 (Ill. 1898).

8. Joseph William Singer, *Property Law as the Infrastructure of Democracy* [The Fourth in the Wolf Family Lecture Series on the American Law of Real Property], 11–1 POWELL ON REAL PROPERTY (2011).

9. *Id.*

10. DONALD L. BARTLETT & MAMES B. STEELE, THE BETRAYAL OF THE AMERICAN DREAM 10–11 (2012); PETER EDELMAN, SO RICH, SO POOR: WHY IT'S SO HARD TO END POVERTY IN AMERICA 32–34 (2012); JOSEPH E. STIGLITZ, THE PRICE OF INEQUALITY: HOW TODAY'S DIVIDED SOCIETY ENDANGERS OUR FUTURE (2012).

11. JOSEPH E. STIGLITZ, THE PRICE OF INEQUALITY: HOW TODAY'S DIVIDED SOCIETY ENDANGERS OUR FUTURE (2012).

12. Aviam Soifer, *Status, Contract, and Promises Unkept*, 96 YALE L. J. 1916, 1939–1945 (1987).

13. Jeremy Waldron, *Homelessness and the Issue of Freedom*, 39 UCLA L. REV. 295 (1991).

14. VIRGINIA WOOLF, A ROOM OF ONE'S OWN (1929), http://ebooks. adelaide.edu.au/w/woolf/virginia/w911/.

15. Joseph William Singer, *Property and Equality: Public Accommodations and the Constitution in South Africa and the United States*, 12 SOUTH AFRICAN J. PUBLIC L. 53 (1997).

16. U.S. CONST. amend. 5; 42 U.S.C. § 1982.

17. 42 U.S.C. § 2000a.

18. 334 U.S. 1 (1948).

19. 42 U.S.C. § 3601 et seq.

20. Joseph William Singer, *The Anti-Apartheid Principle in American Property Law*, 1 Ala. C.R.-C.L. L. Rev. 83 (2011).

21. JOSEPH WILLIAM SINGER, PROPERTY §§ 9.3.1–9.3.2, at 397–409 (4th ed. 2014).

22. JOSEPH WILLIAM SINGER, PROPERTY § 10.5.4, at 472–473 (4th ed. 2014).

23. D.C. CODE § 45–2551; N.J. STAT. §§ 2A:18–61.1 to 2A:18–61.12; JOSEPH WILLIAM SINGER, PROPERTY § 10.5.4, at 472–473 (4th ed. 2014).

24. MASS. GEN. LAWS ch. 186A, §§ 1–6.

25. LAWRENCE M. FRIEDMAN, A HISTORY OF AMERICAN LAW 416 (2d ed. 1985) (describing the Morrill Act of 1862).

26. JOSEPH WILLIAM SINGER, PROPERTY § 2.4.1, at 43–44 (4th ed. 2014).

27. JOSEPH WILLIAM SINGER, PROPERTY § 4.2, at 145–158 (4th ed. 2014).

28. Blakeley v. Gorin, 313 N.E.2d 903 (Mass. 1974).

29. Hawai'i Housing Auth. v. Midkiff, 467 U.S. 229 (1984).

30. 17 U.S.C. § 107.

31. The Proprietors of the Charles River Bridge v. the Proprietors of the Warren Bridge, 36 U.S. 420 (1837); STANLEY I. KUTLER, PRIVILEGE AND CREATIVE DESTRUCTION: THE CHARLES RIVER BRIDGE CASE (1971).

32. People ex rel. Moloney v. Pullman's Palace-Car Co., 51 N.E. 664, 674 (Ill. 1898).

33. Jenn Abelson, *Bostonians Dream Big About a Reborn Downtown Crossing*, BOSTON GLOBE, Feb. 19, 2012; Eliot Brown, *New Tower Would Fill Boston's Scar*, BOSTON GLOBE, Feb. 13, 2012; Thomas Grillo, *Stalled*

Filene's Project Poised for Rebirth, Boston Business J., June 11, 2012; Paul McMorrow, *The Art of the Deal, Boston-style*, Boston Globe, Feb. 7, 2012; Greg Turner, *From Basement to Tower: Condos, Shops Eyed for Downtown Crossing*, Boston Herald, June 12, 2012.

34. Robert Nozick, Anarchy, State, and Utopia 180 (1974).

35. Laura S. Underkuffler, The Idea of Property: Its Meaning and Power 125–27 (2003); Jeremy Waldron, *Homelessness and the Issue of Freedom*, 39 UCLA L. Rev. 295 (1991).

36. Bloch v. Frischholz, 587 F.3d 771 (7th Cir. 2009).

37. *See* Kent Greenfield, *The Unjustified Absence of Federal Fraud Protection in the Labor Market*, 107 Yale L. J. 715 (1997).

38. Christopher L. Peterson, *Foreclosure, Subprime Mortgage Lending, and the Mortgage Electronic Registration System*, 78 U. Cin. L. Rev. 1359, 1364 (2010).

39. Joseph William Singer, *Foreclosure and the Failures of Formality, Or Subprime Mortgage Conundrums and How to Fix Them*, 46 Conn. L. Rev. 497 (2013).

40. Chris Isidore, *Bank of America Sued for Alleged Mortgage Fraud*, @ CNNMoney, Oct. 24, 2012, http://money.cnn.com/2012/10/24/news/companies/bank-of-america-lawsuit/index.html; Jessica Silver-Greenberg, *2 Banks to Settle Case for $417 Million*, N.Y. Times, Nov. 16, 2012; Jessica Silver-Greenberg, *Banks Face Wave of New Mortgage-Securities Suits*, Boston Globe, Dec. 10, 2012.

41. Dale A. Whitman, *A Proposal for a National Mortgage Registry: MERS Done Right*, 78 Mo. L. Rev. 1 (2012).

42. Dale A. Whitman, *A Proposal for a National Mortgage Registry: MERS Done Right*, 78 Mo. L. Rev. 1 (2012).

43. Mortgage Electronic Registration Systems, Inc., www.mersinc.org; Nolan Robinson, *The Case Against Allowing Mortgage Electronic Registrations Systems, Inc. (MERS) to Initiate Foreclosure Proceedings*, 32 Cardozo L. Rev. 1621, 1621–1623 (2011) (explaining the creation of MERS); Alan M. White, *Losing the Paper—Mortgage Assignments, Note Transfers and Consumer Protection*, 24 Loy. Consumer L. Rev. 468, 486 (2012) (explaining how MERS works).

44. *See* Dustin A. Zacks, *Standing in Our Own Sunshine: Reconsidering Standing, Transparency, and Accuracy in Foreclosures*, 29 Quinnipiac L. Rev. 551, 559–585 (2011) (analyzing conflicting theories about MERS's role in the mortgage transactions). *See also* Christopher L. Peterson, *Two Faces: Demystifying the Mortgage Electronic Registration System's*

Land Title Theory, 53 WM. & MARY L. REV. 111, 118–125 (2011) (explaining the problems that arise from these inconsistent claims). *See also* Nolan Robinson, *The Case Against Allowing Mortgage Electronic Registrations Systems, Inc. (MERS) to Initiate Foreclosure Proceedings,* 32 CARDOZO L. REV. 1621, 1645 (2011) ("from a legal standpoint, MERS cannot simultaneous[ly] be both principal and agent").

45. *See* David Waks, *Mortgage Electronic Registration Suspense: What's Happening* (Feb. 1, 2011), http://ssrn.com/abstract=2197135 (detailing myriad foreclosure issues generated by the MERS system).

46. LaSalle Bank Natl. Ass'n v. Lamy, 824 N.Y.S.2d 769, 2006 WL 2251721, at *1 (N.Y. Sup. Ct. 2006) ("only the owner of the note and mortgage at the time of the commencement of a foreclosure action may properly prosecute said action"); Bain v. Metropolitan Mortgage Group, Inc., 285 P.3d 34, 36–37 (Wash. 2012) (because MERS does not hold the note, it can neither initiate nonjudicial foreclosure proceedings nor assign an interest in the note to a trustee who can do so). *Cf.* Mortgage Electronic Registration System, Inc. (MERS) v. Sw. Homes of Ark., 301 S.W.3d 1, 3–5 (Ark. 2009); (MERS has no standing to be involved in foreclosure proceedings because it has no interest in the property and can act as an agent only if directed to do so by a principal); Fed. Home Loan Mortgage Corp. v. Schwartzwald, 979 N.E.2d 1214 (Ohio 2012) (foreclosure action can be brought only by party that is the note beneficiary at the time the action is brought).

47. *See* Andra Ghent, *America's Mortgage Laws in Historical Perspective* (Oct. 24, 2012), available at SSRN: http://ssrn.com/abstract=2166656 (detailing differences among state laws).

48. *See* U.S. Bank Nat'l Ass'n v. Ibanez, 941 N.E.2d 40 (Mass. 2011) (foreclosure improper when bank could not demonstrate clear chain of title to mortgages); Montgomery Cty. v. MERSCORP, Inc., 2012 WL 5199361 (E.D. Pa. 2012) (MERS title system violates Pennsylvania recording statutes); Gretchen Morgenson, *Guilty Pleas in Foreclosure Fraud Cases,* N.Y. TIMES, Nov 21, 2012 (foreclosure processing company founder pleads guilty to charge of fraudulently preparing false documents to evict troubled borrowers from their homes).

49. Joshua J. Card, *Homebuyer Beware: MERS and the Law of Subsequent Purchasers,* 77 BROOK. L. REV. 1163, 1634 (2012).

50. Bain v. Metropolitan Mortgage Group, Inc., 285 P.3d 34, 46 (Wash. 2012) ("MERS offers no authority for the implicit proposition

that the lender's nomination of MERS as a nominee rises to an agency relationship with successor noteholders. MERS fails to identify the entities that control and are accountable for its actions. It has not established that it is an agent for a lawful principal.").

51. *But see* Joshua J. Card, *Homebuyer Beware: MERS and the Law of Subsequent Purchasers,* 77 BROOK. L. REV. 1163, 1662–1663 (2012) (courts should accept MERS as the agent for the current mortgagee); Dustin A. Zacks, MERS *Is Dead: Long Live MERS,* 44 CONNTEMPLATIONS 62, *68 (2012) (arguing that most courts have held MERS to be an agent for the mortgagee and/or note holder or occupies an equivalent status that allows it to act on behalf of the real party in interest).

52. MINN. STAT. § 507.413; Gomes v. Countrywide Home Loans Inc., 121 Cal. Rptr. 3d 819, 826–827 (2011) (MERS may initiate nonjudicial foreclosure under deed of trust); Mortgage Electronic Registration Systems, Inc. v. Revoredo, 955 So. 2d 33, 34 (Fla. Dist. Ct. App. 2007) (MERS may foreclose as agent of the note holder); Residential Funding Co., LLC v. Saurman, 805 N.W.2d 183 (Mich. 2011) (MERS had sufficient "interest in the debt" to initiate nonjudicial foreclosure proceedings); Jackson v. Mortgage Electronic Registration Systems, Inc., 770 N.W.2d 487, 494–495, 501 (Minn. 2009) (applying MINN. STAT. § 507.413 allowing MERS to initiate foreclosure proceedings). *Cf.* Culhane v. Aurora Loan Servs. of Neb., 708 F.3d 282 (1st Cir. 2013) (MERS possesses a legal interest in the mortgage, enabling it to transfer to mortgage to the holder of the beneficial interest or the bank that owns the right to foreclose to secure the underlying debt).

53. LaSalle Bank Natl. Ass'n v. Lamy, 824 N.Y.S.2d 769, 2006 WL 2251721, at *1 (N.Y. Sup. Ct. 2006) ("only the owner of the note and mortgage at the time of the commencement of a foreclosure action may properly prosecute said action"); Bain v. Metropolitan Mortgage Group, Inc., 285 P.3d 34, 36–37 (Wash. 2012) (because MERS does not hold the note, it can neither initiate nonjudicial foreclosure proceedings nor assign an interest in the note to a trustee who can do so). *Cf.* Mortgage Electronic Registration System, Inc. (MERS) v. Sw. Homes of Ark., 301 S.W.3d 1, 3–5 (Ark. 2009); (MERS has no standing to be involved in foreclosure proceedings because it has no interest in the property and can act as an agent only if directed to do so by a principal); Fed. Home Loan Mortgage Corp. v. Schwartzwald, 979 N.E.2d 1214 (Ohio 2012) (foreclosure action can be brought only by party that is the note beneficiary at the time the action is brought).

54. Bank of N.Y. v. Silverberg, 926 N.Y.S.2d 532, 538–539 (App. Div. 2011); LaSalle Bank Nat'l Ass'n v. Lamy, 2006 WL 2251721, at *1–*3 (N.Y. Sup. Ct. 2006). But see In re Relka, 2009 WL 5149262, at *3 (Bankr. D. Wyo. 2009) (MERS has power to assign the note and mortgage).

55. Bank of N.Y. v. Alderazi, 900 N.Y.S.2d 821, 824 (Sup. Ct. 2010) (the "party who claims to be the agent of another bears the burden of proving the agency relationship"). On the difficulty of figuring out when the principal is unclear, see Bain v. Metropolitan Mortgage Group, Inc., 285 P.3d 34, 47–49 (Wash. 2012).

56. In re Maisel, 378 B.R. 19, 22 (Bankr. D. Mass. 2007), quoting In re Parrish, 326 B.R. 708, 720 (Bankr. N.D. Ohio 2005) (agent cannot foreclose without proof of its agency relationship and a showing of the chain of mortgage assignments giving its principal a right to foreclose).

57. Nolan Robinson, *The Case Against Allowing Mortgage Electronic Registrations Systems, Inc. (MERS) to Initiate Foreclosure Proceedings*, 32 Cardozo L. Rev. 1621, 1644 (2011) ("an agent cannot augment or reduce the legal rights of its principal").

58. *See, e.g.*, In re Foreclosure Cases, 521 F.Supp.2d 650 (S.D. Ohio 2007) (no right to foreclose without possession of properly endorsed note); Gee v. U.S. Bank N.A., 72 So. 3d 211, 213–214 (Fla. Dist. Ct. App. 2011) (assignee of a mortgage cannot foreclose when it failed to establish how its predecessor became the successor in interest to the prior holder of the mortgage); Deutsche Bank Natl. Trust v. Mitchell, 27 A.3d 1229 (N.J. Super. Ct. App. Div. 2011) (same); Alan M. White, *Losing the Paper—Mortgage Assignments, Note Transfers and Consumer Protection*, 24 Loy. Consumer L. Rev. 468, 474–477 (2012) (sloppy treatment of notes was widespread, making it difficult for lenders to show properly endorsed notes to prove they had a right to foreclose); *id.* at 495 (noting the "extensive inaccuracy of MERS" records). *See also* Bradley T. Borden, David J. Reiss, & KeAupuni Akina, *Show Me the Note!* 19 Westlaw J. Bank & Lender Liability 1 (June 3, 2013) (discussing competing state court rulings on the question of whether foreclosure can be avoided if the foreclosing party cannot produce the note on which the mortgage is based.

59. Bevilacqua v. Rodriguez, 955 N.E.2d 884, 893–897 (Mass. 2011) (if nonjudicial foreclosure is invalid because the foreclosing party could not prove it possessed the right to foreclose, then the

purchaser at the foreclosure sale cannot transfer good title to a third party); U.S. Bank Nat'l Ass'n v. Ibanez, 941 N.E.2d 40, 49–51 (Mass. 2011) (foreclosure is invalid unless the foreclosing party proved a right to possession of the property before the foreclosure occurred, so subsequent purchaser could not prove that it acquired good title sufficient to claims rights against the current possessor).

60. MERS's website takes the contradictory positions that MERS is the "original mortgagee" and that it is the "agent" for the "owner of the loan" as well as the "mortgage lender." This waffling in legal positions is part of what has confused the courts about what MERS's legal status is. See http://www.mersinc.org/about-us/faq.

61. David E. Woolley & Lisa D. Herzog, MERS: The Unreported Effects of Lost Chain of Title on Real Property Owners, 8 HASTINGS BUS. L. J. 365, 367 (2012) (MERS may make various titles unmarketable).

62. Robert C. Hockett, Paying Paul and Robbing No One: An Eminent Domain Solution for Underwater Mortgage Debt That Can Benefit Literally Everyone, Cornell Law School research paper No. 12–64, at 6–7, http://ssrn.com/abstract=2173358.

63. Alan M. White, Losing the Paper—Mortgage Assignments, Note Transfers and Consumer Protection, 24 LOY. CONSUMER L. REV. 468, 469–470 (2012).

64. Chase Home Finance, LLC v. Fequiere, 989 A.2d 606, 611 (Conn. App. Ct. 2010); Alan M. White, Losing the Paper—Mortgage Assignments, Note Transfers and Consumer Protection, 24 LOY. CONSUMER L. REV. 468, 489 (2012); RESTATEMENT (THIRD) OF PROPERTY (MORTGAGES) § 5.4(c) ("A mortgage may be enforced only by, or in behalf of, a person who is entitled to enforce the obligation the mortgage secures.").

65. Saxon Mortgage Services, Inc. v. Hillery, 2008 WL 5170180, at *5 (N.D. Cal. 2008) (quoting Carpenter v. Longan, 83 U.S. [16 Wall.] 271, 274 [1872]).

66. Chase Home Finance, LLC v. Fequiere, 989 a.2d 606, 610–612 (Conn. App. Ct. 2010) (proper holder of the note may foreclose even if it has not been assigned the mortgage) (applying CONN. GEN. STAT. § 49–17); Mortgage Electronic Registration Systems, Inc. v. Coakley, 838 N.Y.S.2d 622, 623 (App. Div. 2007). Note also that a party may hold the note for the benefit of another party and act as an agent for that party, thus occupying a status as a "person entitled to enforce the note" although the proceeds of any such enforcement action

belong to the principal who "owns" the note. BAC Home Loans Servicing v. Kolenich, 2012 WL 5306059, ¶ 39 (Ohio Ct. App. 2012) (mortgage can be foreclosed by holder of a negotiable note, even if the note is "owned" by a different party); Joshua J. Card, *Homebuyer Beware: MERS and the Law of Subsequent Purchasers*, 77 BROOK L. REV. 1633, 1651 (2012) (New York law grants primary rights to the note holder).

67. Crum v. LaSalle Bank, N.A, 55 So.3d 266, 269 (Ala. Civ. App. 2009); Wells Fargo Bank, N.A. v. Marchione, 69 A.D.3d 204, 209, 887 N.Y.S.2d 615 (App. Div. 2009); Wells Fargo Bank, N.A. v. Byrd, 897 N.E.2d 722 723 (Ohio Ct. App. 2008).

68. In re Agard, 444 B.R. 231, 254 (Bankr. E.D. N.Y. 2011); Eaton v. Federal Nat'l Mortgage Ass'n, 969 N.E.2d 1118, 1121 (Mass. 2012).

69. On the complexity of the issues involved in determining the relation between the note and the mortgage see Adam Levitin, *The Paper Chase: Securitization, Foreclosure, and the Uncertainty of Mortgage Title*, 63 DUKE L. J. 637 (2013) (explaining the ambiguities in Article 3 and Article 9); Note, *Consumer Law—Mortgage Foreclosure—Massachusetts Supreme Judicial Court Unanimously Voids Foreclosure Sales Because Securitization Trusts Could Not Demonstrate Clear Chains of Title—U.S. Bank Nat'l Ass'n v. Ibanez*, 941 N.E. 2d 40 (Mass. 2001), 125 HARV. L. REV. 827, 831–833 (2011).

70. For a detailed explanation of various title problems MERS created, see David E. Woolley & Lisa D. Herzog, *MERS: The Unreported Effects of Lost Chain of Title on Real Property Owners*, 8 HASTINGS BUS. L. J. 365, 367 (2012).

71. Joseph William Singer, *Democratic Estates: Property Law in a Free and Democratic Society*, 94 CORNELL L. REV. 1009,1023 (2009) (traditional core of property law is the promotion of alienability); Joseph William Singer, *The Rule of Reason in Property Law*, 46 U.C. DAVIS L. REV. 1369 (2013) (property law aims to achieve clear titles).

72. Montgomery Cty. v. MERSCORP, Inc., 2012 WL 5199361 (E.D. Pa. 2012) (interpreting Pennsylvania statutes, 21 PENN. STAT. § 351, to require recording for transfers of interests in land to be valid). Cf. PHH Mortg. Serv. Corp. v. Perreira, 200 P.3d 1180, 1186 (Idaho 2008), interpreting IDAHO CODE § 45-1505 (trustee cannot foreclose on a trust deed unless it and any assignments of the trust deed are recorded); Hooker v. Northwest Trustee Services, 2011 WL 2119103 (D. Or. 2011), interpreting OR. REV. STAT. § 86.735 (nonjudicial

foreclosure not available in Oregon unless all mortgage assignments are recorded).

73. MERS's website misleadingly asserts that it does not "hide the mortgage note owner" because all MERS mortgages "are recorded in the public land records" while acknowledging that the purpose of the MERS system is to make it unnecessary for lenders to record mortgage assignments. "Because MERS is a common agent for its members, recording an assignment of the mortgage is not necessary when ownership of the promissory note or servicing rights transfer between members." http://www.mersinc.org/about-us/faq. *See also* Christopher L. Peterson, *Foreclosure, Subprime Mortgage Lending, and the Mortgage Electronic Registration System*, 78 U. CIN. L. REV. 1359, 1400–1404 (2010) (noting the negative effect of MERS on public land title records).

74. Tanya Marsh, *Foreclosures and the Failure of the American Title Recording System*, 111 COLUM. L. REV. SIDEBAR 19, 23 (2011).

75. Nolan Robinson, *The Case Against Allowing Mortgage Electronic Registrations Systems, Inc. (MERS) to Initiate Foreclosure Proceedings*, 32 CARDOZO L. REV. 1621,1638 (2011).

76. Tanya Marsh, *Foreclosures and the Failure of the American Title Recording System*, 111 COLUM. L. REV. SIDEBAR 19, 23 (2011). Complaint, Comm. of Mass. v. Bank of America ¶ 150(b), Civ. A. No. 11–4363 (Dec. 1, 2011), http://www.mass.gov/ago/docs/press/ag-complaint-national-banks.pdf.

77. Adam J. Levitin & Tara Twomey, *Mortgage Servicing*, 28 YALE J. ON REGULATION 1 (2011) (analyzing servicer incentives).

78. KATHLEEN C. ENGEL & PATRICIA A. McCOY, THE SUBPRIME VIRUS: RECKLESS CREDIT, REGULATORY FAILURE, AND NEXT STEPS 131 (2011); 131; Alan M. White, *Losing the Paper—Mortgage Assignments, Note Transfers and Consumer Protection*, 24 LOY. CONSUMER L. REV. 468, 496 (2012).

79. *See, e.g.*, Abraham Bell & Gideon Parchomovsky, *Reconfiguring Property in Three Dimensions*, 75 U. CHI. L. REV. 1015, 1022 (2008) ("There cannot be ownership in land without some clear idea of who owns the land, what land is owned, and what rights accrue to the owner as a result of her status."); Steven J. Eagle, *Private Property, Development and Freedom: On Taking Our Own Advice*, 59 SMU L. REV. 345, 352 (2006) ("Individuals working to grow their assets must be supported by clear laws defining their property rights.").

80. Henry E. Smith, *Exclusion v. Governance: Two Strategies for Delineating Property Rights*, 31 J. LEGAL STUD. 453 (2002); Henry E. Smith, *Property and Property Rules*, 79 NYU L. REV. 1719, 1797 (2004) ("Property rules have informational advantages").

81. Henry E. Smith, *Property as the Law of Things*, 125 HARV. L. REV. 1691, 1691, 1698, 1700–1713 (2012).

82. Joseph William Singer, *The Rule of Reason in Property Law*, 46 U.C. DAVIS L. REV. 1369 (2013).

83. Nolan Robinson, *The Case Against Allowing Mortgage Electronic Registrations Systems, Inc. (MERS) to Initiate Foreclosure Proceedings*, 32 CARDOZO L. REV. 1621, 1635–1636 (2011); Alan M. White, *Losing the Paper—Mortgage Assignments, Note Transfers and Consumer Protection*, 24 LOY. CONSUMER L. REV. 468, 494–496 (2012).

84. MICH. COMP. LAWS § 600.3204(3); Timothy A. Froehle, *Standing in the Wake of the Foreclosure Crisis: Why Procedural Requirements Are Necessary to Prevent Further Loss to Homeowners*, 96 IOWA L. REV. 1719, 1740 (2011) (recommending adoption of this requirement by other states).

85. Laura A. Steven, *MERS and the Mortgage Crisis: Obfuscating Loan Ownership and the Need for Clarity*, 7 BROOK. J. CORP. FIN. & COM. L. 251, 270 (2012) (arguing for federal legislation to require MERS to open its records to the public); Alan M. White, *Losing the Paper—Mortgage Assignments, Note Transfers and Consumer Protection*, 24 LOY. CONSUMER L. REV. 468, 497 (2012) (advocating full disclosure of agency relationships and transfer history); Dustin A. Zacks, *Standing in Our Own Sunshine: Reconsidering Standing, Transparency, and Accuracy in Foreclosures*, 29 QUINNIPIAC L. REV. 551, 607–608 (2011) (arguing for greater public transparency in MERS records). Note that the Truth in Lending Act (TILA) was amended to require homeowners to be notified of changes in beneficial ownership of loans. Dustin A. Zacks, *Standing in Our Own Sunshine: Reconsidering Standing, Transparency, and Accuracy in Foreclosures*, 29 QUINNIPIAC L. REV. 551, 593–594 (2011) (citing Helping Families Save Their Homes Act of 2009, Pub. L. No. 111–22, § 404, 123 Stat 1632, 1658 (2009); 15 U.S.C. § 1641).

86. Alan M. White, *Losing the Paper—Mortgage Assignments, Note Transfers and Consumer Protection*, 24 LOY. CONSUMER L. REV. 468, 497 (2012).

87. Dale A. Whitman, *Are We There Yet? The Case for a Uniform Electronic Recording Act*, 24 W. N. ENG. L. REV. 245 (2002).

88. Dale A. Whitman, *A Proposal for a National Mortgage Registry: MERS Done Right*, 78 Mo. L. Rev. 1 (2012).

89. Adam Levitin, *The Paper Chase: Securitization, Foreclosure, and the Uncertainty of Mortgage Title*, 63 Duke L. J. 637 (2013); Alan M. White, *Losing the Paper—Mortgage Assignments, Note Transfers and Consumer Protection*, 24 Loy. Consumer L. Rev. 468, 498 (2012).

90. Dustin A. Zacks, *Standing in Our Own Sunshine: Reconsidering Standing, Transparency, and Accuracy in Foreclosures*, 29 Quinnipiac L. Rev. 551, 554 (2011).

91. Tanya Marsh, *Foreclosures and the Failure of the American Title Recording System*, 111 Colum. L. Rev. Sidebar 19, 24–26 (2011). David Waks has similarly advocated for the creation of an independent federal agency to fulfill this role. David Waks, *Mortgage Electronic Registration Suspense: What's Happening* 32 (Feb. 1, 2011), http://ssrn.com/abstract=2197135.

5.
Why Conservatives Like Regulation and Liberals Like Markets

1. Ringside Seat, American Prospect, Feb. 25, 2013, http://www.e-activist.com/ea-campaign/action.handleViewInBrowser.do?ea.campaigner.email=CqwWVGSGUygp%2F0B1KKe%2FDJdM2S9onP51&broadcastId=24859&templateId=17542.

2. *See, e.g.*, Brian Barry, Why Social Justice Matters (2005).

6.
Democratic Liberty

1. John Locke, The Second Treatise of Government ¶ 57, at 306 (Peter Laslett ed., 1988, Cambridge Univ. Press, 2009 reprinting) (original 1690) (italics in original).

2. Max Barry, Jennifer Government (2003).

Acknowledgments

Many people have made this book possible. First to thank are the many scholars and lawyers I have conversed with over the years on these topics. An inevitably incomplete list includes David Abromowitz, Greg Alexander, John Arnholz, Bethany Berger, Roger Bertling, Kevin Costello, David Dana, Nestor Davidson, Rashmi Dyal-Chand, Kathleen Engel, Kent Greenfield, David Grossman, Andy Kaufman, Adam Levitin, Jeremy McClane, Eduardo Peñalver, Jed Purdy, Sabeel Rahman, John Rattigan, John Savarese, Laura Underkuffler, André van der Walt, Johan van der Walt, Sjef van Erp, Rachael Walsh, Emma Waring, Max Weinstein, Alan White, and Dale Whitman.

Research for this book has been supported for many years by grants from Harvard Law School. I would also like to thank the participants in the Progressive Property Conferences held at Harvard Law School in May 2012 and at Tulane Law School in May 2013. Parts of this book were presented in a different form at the Master Class following the Young Property Lawyers Forum at Stellenbosch University, South Africa, in October 2012, hosted by the South African Research Chair in Property Law, held by André van der Walt. Aspects of this book were also presented at the University of Luxembourg in April 2013 and at a faculty workshop at U.C. Davis School of Law in September 2013. The book in its present form also benefits from the feedback from the faculty of

Boston College Law School at a faculty workshop in February 2014. I am very grateful to the participants of all these conferences and workshops for their helpful comments and suggestions.

Parts of this book previously appeared in an altered form in the following articles:

> *Property as the Law of Democracy*, 63 Duke L.J. 1287 (2014)
>
> *Foreclosure and the Failures of Formality, Or Subprime Mortgage Conundrums and How to Fix Them*, 46 Conn. L. Rev. 497 (2013)
>
> *The Rule of Reason in Property Law*, 46 U.C. Davis L. Rev. 1369 (2013)
>
> *Subprime: Why a Free and Democratic Society Needs Law*, 47 Harv. C.R.-C. L. L. Rev. 141 (2012)
>
> *Property Law as the Infrastructure of Democracy [The Fourth in the Wolf Family Lecture Series on the American Law of Real Property]*, 11-1 Powell on Real Property (2011)
>
> *The Anti-Apartheid Principle in American Property Law*, 1 Ala. C.R.-C.L. L. Rev. 83 (2011)
>
> *Property Law and the Mortgage Crisis: Libertarian Fantasies and Subprime Realities*, 1 Prop. L. Rev. 7 (2011)
>
> *Democratic Estates: Property Law in a Free and Democratic Society*, 94 Cornell L. Rev. 1009 (2009)
>
> *Corporate Responsibility in a Free and Democratic Society*, 58 Case W. Res. L. Rev. 1031 (2008)

Acknowledgments

Family members who took the time and care to give me their thoughts over the years were Martha Minow, Mira Singer, Lila Singer, and Newton Minow. Without their love and support, I would not have been free to think, wonder, and work, and this book would never have seen the light of day.

Index

adjustable rate mortgages, 78,
   81, 136
adverse possession, 105–6, 110,
   120
Affordable Care Act
   ("Obamacare"), 3
alienability, 41, 43, 97, 112, 121;
   as core value, 149; feudal
   obstacles to, 38, 39–40;
   information essential to, 146,
   147, 150, 152
anarchism, 3, 6
antidiscrimination laws. See
   civil rights laws
antifeudalism, 44–51, 54, 68, 96,
   99, 127, 162, 173, 175, 178
apartheid, 100, 101
aristocracy, 20
associational freedom, 48, 128

bankruptcy, 17, 113
Barry, Max, 180–81
Bartlett, Randall, 107–8
Battle of Hastings (1066), 32
behavioral economics, 90
Bentham, Jeremy, 15, 95
Berkeley, John, 36, 37, 38, 55
blight, 117, 119
Boaz, David, 185 n. 20
Boehner, John, 184 n. 12
border disputes, 105–6, 167

Boston, 116–18
building codes, 121, 162;
   advantages of, 66, 72; cost of,
   75–76, 88; fairness of, 82;
   libertarian objections to,
   63–64, 86
Burke, Edmund, 177

California, 104
Cantor, Eric, 184 n. 12
Carteret, George, 36, 37
Carteret, Philip, 36, 37, 38, 55
caveat emptor, 60, 61, 65, 80,
   173
Charles II, King of England, 36,
   98
*Charles River Bridge v. Warren
   Bridge* (1837), 110
civil forfeiture, 112
Civil Rights Act (1866), 102
civil rights laws, 46, 48–49, 50,
   158, 162, 164, 188 n. 41
Civil War, 45
Clean Air Act (1970), 70
Clean Water Act (1972), 70
coal mining, 70–71
common law, 34, 44, 74,
   122–28
community property, 102–3
condominiums, 51–52, 99, 111,
   121, 167

Index